Two Journeys

The outer journey working with abandoned
children in Romania between 1996 and 1998

The inner journey discovering
how God interacts with our lives

by

Caroline Lucas

**Grosvenor House
Publishing Limited**

This book is published by
Grosvenor House Publishing Ltd
28-30 High Street, Guildford, Surrey, GU1 3EL.
www.grosvenorhousepublishing.co.uk

A CIP record for this book
is available from the British Library

ISBN 978-1-78623-914-3

Some names and identifying details have been
changed to protect the privacy of individuals

PROLOGUE

Take heed that you despise not one of these little ones:
for I say unto you, That in heaven their angels do always
behold the face of my Father that is in heaven

Matthew18 v10.

CONTENTS

Chapters 1-3   How it all started

Chapters 4-12   Braila

Chapters 13-19   Harja

Chapters 20-end   The breakthrough, hope at last

HOW IT ALL STARTED

CHAPTER ONE

In 1996 when I was 59, everything in my life changed. Not in an obvious outward way but in an extraordinary inner way. It started when my son Sam persuaded me, somewhat reluctantly, to say a prayer led by him.

I had not come from a Christian family, and though I was christened as a baby I don't remember us ever going to church. I had been in a church, as I had occasionally been taken to church by an elderly friend of our family. At one time my brother Bruv, who was 8 years older than me, started going to Church on his own, but he never talked about it; it was as if it was a personal and private thing. As a family we never talked about God as the whole subject seemed rather embarrassing. Neither did I take any of my children to church.

When Sam was in his early 20s he suddenly announced that he had become a Christian. We did not at first take him too seriously, we had seen Sam follow many enthusiasms. He had been for a while a traveller, living in a covered cart pulled by a strong piebald horse, travelling the country, stopping in lay-byes to cook over a small fire. Then he had been to India twice looking for answers, and at one time he called himself a Buddhist. So this latest enthusiasm seemed like something that would eventually pass away as the others had.

The only thing was that this was such an all consuming passion – we joked that whatever subject we mentioned, Sam would bring it back to God.

I was pleased for him but did not for a moment consider it for myself.

As the years passed Sam went to live in Plymouth. He married Katie, who had also become a Christian, and they had two boys. Then when my youngest son Ben became ill it seemed clear to Sam that he needed spiritual help and so he persuaded Ben to join them in Plymouth. I won't tell Ben's story but the upshot was that months later when Ben was back in North Devon he told me he too had become a Christian. Again I was pleased for him but again did not feel personally tempted.

I remembered how years before I had been living in Winchelsea with a broken marriage and three young children. Fanny and Joe were 7 and 6, and went to the local primary school, and because I worked part time, Sam who was 2, went to Miss Rosling's nursery school in Rye, and because I did not drive I paid a girl from the nearby secondary school to bring him back with her in the bus. One day when I was feeling desperately unhappy I went into the Church. It was thankfully empty, and I knelt down and prayed "What must I do?" expecting no answer, then I heard in my head the words "Meet Sam off the bus" I suddenly realised what the time was, I had been so absorbed by my own unhappiness I had not realised it was so late. I just had time to run out of the church as the bus appeared around the corner.

I found this enormously comforting, I felt certain the prompting had not been my thought as it had taken me by surprise, and I put it down to some sort of guardian angel. I thought that God might after all be real, and decided to find out more about it. So I asked the dear old Rector of the nearby village of Icklesham, to prepare me for confirmation. I went to him rather than the unknown Winchelsea vicar, because he owned the house I rented, and before we moved in he and his wife had walked over to the empty house to pray.

I did not tell him about the voice, and I am afraid I don't remember anything of the teaching, and after it was over I went just once to the large unfriendly Winchelsea Church. The service was from King James, the congregation was elderly, and I felt like a complete outsider. and I found myself becoming angry because nothing there seemed relevant to my life. So I decided that this was not for me and never went to a church service again.

Time passed... Now with hindsight I can see that God had touched my life long before I became a Christian, I had even acknowledged it then as being something special, and again I had wondered if there were guardian angels that looked after us in some way.

Once, walking along a road near my sister's house, thinking of nothing special, I suddenly heard a voice in my head say very clearly

"God is love." That was all.

Now I had heard this phrase before, and had always dismissed it as the sort of soppy thing that Christians say – but this time I was completely confounded. So much so that I remember every detail of where I was at the time – the street – the low wall – the houses – and I knew that this was not a phrase it was the TRUTH. I knew with every part of me that this was literally the truth. God is Love. And for a while, (about two days), I seemed to understand this truth, and then the understanding slipped away. I tried to cling onto it, even tried to write it down, but it was no use. However, what I was left with was the certain knowledge that it was still there, even if I could no longer understand it in the same way, I knew that it had not been my own thought – It was something outside myself which had shown me briefly a great truth.

I remembered how another earlier time I had also heard this voice. It was when my husband, Peter, and I were living in a cottage in the country with our three young children. Everyone was out and I was alone. I had a little Mallard duckling that had been found at the side of the road and had been given to me to rear as we kept ducks. I kept him in the house as the other ducks bullied him, and this day I decided to introduce him to water and took him out and stood him on a brick in the children's paddling pool. He was nervous at first and then suddenly got the idea and began to swim around very fast and excitedly. It was great fun kneeling there enjoying his antics, and then I heard a gentle voice in my head say something like.

"Enjoy this time. Don't waste it thinking about the future. Enjoy *now*, because one day you will look back on this as a very happy time"

I was amazed, and realised that I had got into the habit of supposing that things would be better when the children were a bit older…when we had a car instead of just two bicycles… when we had a bit more money.. …when…when… I knew it had not been my thoughts that had spoken – it was something outside myself. It was not an angry or reproving voice, it was just gently pointing out something I was missing.

The following winter Peter fell in love with our friend Jane and our marriage catastrophically collapsed. I remembered the voice, or what I thought was a guardian angel, and in some way it helped me during that awful time.

Two days after Peter told me he and Jane were in love I had to go to the Christmas concert at Fanny's school. She was 5. I gathered up 4 year old Joe and baby Sam and then as I got to the school the most gentle peace filled me – a calm loving stillness – and I sat through the performance enveloped in this protective peace. All the tears and talk and exhaustion were washed away. This gentle support lasted about two and a half days and then gradually faded, but as the unhappiness flooded back I was again helped.

We had a vegetable stand in the corner of our kitchen and in one of the baskets was a red cabbage. It had been there so long that it was black and shrivelled, and as my eye fell on it I noticed that where the stem had been cut there were little shoots growing. These leaves were as small and delicate as rose petals, and were a soft green tinged with pink and as I looked at them I felt hope. It was as if I was being shown that even something as dead, dark and hopeless as that cabbage could send out these beautiful little shoots and it seemed like a promise that life is not always as dark as it seemed.

CHAPTER TWO

To return to 1996, to when Sam led me through a simple prayer asking God to forgive me for the things I had done wrong in my life and asking him to come into my life. I said it after Sam and did not feel anything, just a slight sense of disappointment because in spite of my pessimism, there had been a faint hidden hope that something might change. Sam went off, and Ben and Elke, his girlfriend, were travelling in Chile, and so I was alone.

I was quite happy living on the coast in North Devon. I had a pottery to run and also a holiday cottage that I let, and I kept busy and almost forgot about my prayer with Sam. Then I read an article in the Sunday Times about a wonderful man who had started 'The Medical Foundation for the Care of Victims of Torture'. It was an inspiring article and I could not get it out of my mind – so much so that I began to think of offering them my holiday cottage as a place to recover. I worked out that I could manage to live on my earnings in the pottery and the basic government pension which I would start getting in January when I was 60. So I wrote to the man and offered him my holiday cottage telling him it could accommodate eight people and was fully equipped with everything needed down to the last teaspoon. I could offer it rent free but would not be able to pay the rates and expenses like water and electricity. After a while he wrote back graciously declining as they could not afford any expenses and it was too far from London.

At about this time I began to have some dreams. They were different from my usual dreams which vanished as I woke up. These felt completely real and they had a common theme. In all of them I had the care of a small vulnerable child and I could feel that the situation was not safe or benign – I knew it was not my child, but I had to protect it.

It was a different child in each dream but the sense of threat and urgency was the same, and these dreams were so real, that when I woke up I would start to search anxiously around the bed for the child until I realised it was just a dream.

Then all day the dream would linger and the sense of urgency did not go. These dreams did not come every night, but enough to make me disturbed because they made me feel that I should be doing something but did not know what. Finally, in desperation I went to a bible.

I had never read the bible so did not know where to look, and opened it at random to see if there might be an answer there. It opened at the front, and the passage my eye fell on made no connection so I tried again in the middle – again nothing – so for the last time I opened it near the end and read the first thing I saw.

It was John 21 verses15-18 and was the passage when Jesus speaks to Peter after his resurrection.

'When they had finished eating, Jesus said to Simon Peter "Simon, son of John, do you truly love me more than these?"
"Yes Lord" He said, "You know that I love you."
Jesus said "Feed my lambs"
Again Jesus said, "Simon, son of John, do you truly love me?"
He answered, "Yes Lord, you know I love you."
Jesus said "Take care of my sheep."
The third time he said to him. "Simon, son of John, do you love me?
Peter was hurt because Jesus asked him the third time, "Do you love me?" He said "Lord, you know all things, you know that I love you"

Jesus said, "Feed my sheep."

I did not know the background, but as I read it I felt all the hairs on my arms and neck stand up. The command "Feed my lambs" seemed to be directly spoken to me – three times he said it and I was very moved – but how did he mean me to do it?

For a few days I pondered about it while the feeling of urgency grew. I found myself pacing around the house making little grunting noises as I tried to understand.

The strange thing was that I knew about feeding lambs – literally. When we had a farm I had reared orphan lambs collected from the lamb bank and I had become completely absorbed with the best way to do it. I had been warned by a farmers wife when I collected the first one, that most hand reared lambs died quite quickly. So I studied the constitution of sheep's milk and found it was twice as concentrated as cow's milk, and I found that the calves' powdered milk was right for my lambs if I used half the amount of water and fed them little and often and made sure the temperature was just right, and they thrived.

Once, when some of our hoggets and their lambs got pneumonia I had milked the young mothers by hand, and then used a tube to stomach feed their lambs with their mother's milk, doing this every three hours, day and night. I remembered how one stormy night in March I had crawled out of bed and had put on boots and a coat over my nightdress and had gone out to the building where the sheep were housed. I climbed over the rail and milked the skittish mother (she was getting better) and then picked up her lamb that lay under a hot lamp and began to tube feed it. It was still and quiet inside but the storm was raging outside, and I began to automatically think that it was quite an ordeal having to keep doing this in the middle of the night, when suddenly I realised it was exactly the opposite – because I absolutely loved it. I adored caring for these lambs and was completely absorbed doing it.

Now, with the bible in my hand, I felt as if I was being told to do it again. Jesus had said 'lambs and sheep' but he had not meant Peter to do that literally. By 'lambs' he had meant vulnerable people, and that was what I was being told to do. But how?

This incident made me realise two things – both of them rather surprising – one was that God seemed to have a sense of humour; the last thing I expected. And the other was that he must have been with me throughout my life even though I was not a Christian. This was rather a daunting thought.

I decided to talk to our vicar, David Ford. I had met him once when he first took over our parish. He had called at the pottery to introduce himself, and he had seemed a nice sort of man and not intimidating. So I gave him a ring and asked if I could come over and see him about something. As I sat in his study I explained about The Medical Foundation for the Care of victims of Torture and my hopes for using Chapel Cottage. We had a long discussion, first about that, and then about God, and I found him very easy to talk to. So eventually I plucked up courage and told him about my dreams. He listened and did not seem surprised or sceptical and I realised that he did not think it was at all odd that God sometimes sends us dreams, even to someone like me who was not a Christian. It was such a relief to be able to talk so openly with someone, and next Sunday I decided to go to Church.

The parish church was across the valley from me, overlooking the sea, and it was a pleasant wooded walk down the lane to reach it. I found that they were using the same King James Service book that had made me feel so alien and angry thirty years before, but this time, as we spoke those ancient words, I found the tears were pouring down my cheeks and dripping off my chin. I was so moved, but I did not know why – it was as if some unconscious part of myself was responding in a way I could not understand. The next Sunday I was welcomed by the small, mostly elderly, congregation, and so I continued going every Sunday.

I was invited by David to join their home group at the vicarage where I met his lovely wife Shiela, (who was to become a very special friend). And a few other people. We sang some songs, none of which I knew, and had some prayer and teaching. Gradually I was feeling my way into being a committed Christian. As I grew to know the others I began to realise that there was far more to them than I could ever have guessed. It was a lesson I would have to learn again and again – to never judge anyone by their outside. I had not realised to what extent I was selective about other people, as I was so often shown that someone I would have previously dismissed as being boring, surprised and humbled me by their openness and depths of insight.

David had started contacting children's homes to see if any of them needed to use Chapel Cottage for their charges, but weeks went by and nothing turned up. Meanwhile the dreams went on, not nearly as frequent but still as urgent. I had started going on an Alpha course and began reading the Bible and also Christian writers like C S Lewis and Adrian Plass, so different from each other but both very readable. It was as if I had discovered a hole in myself that needed filling.

CHAPTER THREE

One day, talking with David, we began to wonder whether it was not my house that God wanted, it was me.

The next week David handed me a leaflet that had been sent to him. It was about an orphanage in Romania. Now I knew nothing about Romania. I'm afraid that when a programme came on the television about the dreadful orphanages I had quickly changed channels. I did not want to see suffering when there was nothing I could do about it.

But I read the leaflet. It was by a few girls who had been working in a British run hospice in Chernaboda and who decided, when they had some free days, to look up a child they had grown fond of and who had been returned to an orphanage in Braila in the far East of Romania. When they got there they were appalled by what they saw.

At that time, though there was growing concern about the large number of children in the standard orphanages in Romania, it was not generally known what happened to the children who had failed to meet certain arbitrary criteria and so had been sent to orphanages for the 'irricupables.' Braila's sectia RMPSC was one of these orphanages. The girls told the director, Dr Stefan, that they would like to help, and so they organised supplies of clothes, toothpaste and toys, but as well they offered to come and help personally. So two of them left the Hospice and moved to Braila to help however they could. The leaflet was to raise money to support this work. At the bottom was a London telephone number.

I rang this number and was told that Penny was away visiting her mother. I asked where that was and was told

"In Devon"

"Where in Devon?"

"Bideford"

Extraordinary – This was my local town. I rang the number she gave me and got Penny who suggested I come and meet her and see their video. I left at once and half an hour later I had met Penny and was watching a video of the two of the girls doing what they could to relieve the children's suffering. And I knew with total certainty that this was where I must go.

Penny said that they had been praying for someone to turn up, as Susan, one of the girls there, was leaving to marry a Romanian and the other girl, Anthea, would not be able to stay on her own. I asked Penny how much it might cost to work there for a year and she said about seven thousand pounds.

Back home I considered this sum. I had no savings, just my income from the pottery and the holiday cottage. I contacted my letting agents and asked what monthly rent I could ask for Chapel Cottage with a permanent tenant, she told me, and then I remembered the state pension was due to start in January when I turned 60. And so I added twelve times the cottage rent and 52 times my pension and found it came to exactly the sum Jenny had said. Now I was certain that God was organising this move. It felt as if doors were opening, because within two hours of reading the leaflet, I had watched the video, discussed going out with Penny and now the money seemed alright, but the most convincing thing was my instant recognition that this was where I had to go. These children were my lambs that I had been told to look after.

David and Shiela were very supportive and so were Ben and Elke when they returned from Chile. Elke had also become a Christian and they were now engaged. It was agreed that they would live in my cottage and run the pottery while I was away.

Then followed a busy time, I had to get Chapel Cottage ready for a permanent tenant after the last holiday tenants had left. And I was able to fly out to Romania for two weeks to meet Anthea and Susan, and to go with them into the orphanage – though in a way it seemed immaterial as I knew I would be going there whatever it was like.

The girls rented a two room apartment in one of the square grey concrete 'blocs' that had gone up during the communist era. They shared the larger living room and I slept on a mattress on the floor of the one bedroom.

Each morning we walked to the orphanage, it took forty minutes. We walked through the main town to where the roads became rough and the houses were shabby wooden shacks, then down a muddy track to a building standing alone. It looked like a factory and was square with large windows that were shuttered on the inside. We rang the doorbell and were let in and immediately went into a small locked room off the hall. This was officially the isolation room but had never been used as such and was now used by the girls. It was stuffed with all the toys and equipment that they had managed to collect and bring out; boxes of toys of all sorts. There were a couple of chairs, a bed, a ball pool and children's chairs. We put on brightly patterned overalls and gathered up a few toys and went upstairs to the main salon.

The first impression was the smell. Though it was November and cold outside, inside the radiators were covered with wet washing and the damp atmosphere was infiltrated with the heavy scent of urine and faeces as none of the children had access to a lavatory and none wore nappies. We approached a group of children who were sitting squashed up on a mat, they were dressed in rags and some had shaven heads, and as we approached they surged towards us and began to pull at our clothes; reaching up imploringly, watched by an impassive faced Romanian woman who sat holding a stick in her hand. As Anthea and Susan pushed past she began to threaten the children with her stick until they all scuttled back onto the mat where they rocked aimlessly, or sucked their wrists or crawled over each other. There was a black and white television which the woman watched; keeping her stick poised should any children stray off the mat.

The girls went into a side salon lined with cots. Some had larger active children lying with their wrists and ankles tied tightly to the cots bars. Others held up to three children lying weakly. The girls began lifting out some of these children and laying them on bean bags or on the plastic covered foam mats on the floor. They told me that all the equipment in the room had been provided by them – before it had contained nothing but the concrete floor, the cots, and a metal table and a sink.

We did what we could to relieve their suffering as some of the more immobile ones had oozing sores where they lay on soiled mattresses. We gave others rattles to shake or other simple babies' toys. It was clear that though these children were not babies they had no more idea how to play with toys than a baby would.

After a while the girls each chose one child from the three salons and carried them down to the playroom where they could try to give them whatever help they needed.

I was particularly struck by a beautiful boy called Alin who was allowed to wander around aimlessly playing with a strip of bandage. He was very slim and I was surprised to be told he was ten years old.

I realised that there was some pattern to the children's lives, those too weak to sit up spent all their time in the cots. Also in the cots, but tied hand and foot were those too active to be restrained on the mat, while some of the older, biddable children went down to a lower salon, (what happened there I never found out) and just a few, like Alin; who were completely passive and lived in a world of their own were free to move around unrestrained. I was told that Alin always regurgitated his food after a meal but no one seemed bothered and he was not offered any additional food or helped in any way.

At noon someone came with a tray of tin cups half full of a watery mush of potatoes, cabbage or carrots and a stack of bottles for those unable to eat, and an impatient member of the staff would prop a bottle into the mouths of all those lying in the cots, and then shovel the contents of the cups into the eager mouths of all the others.

I noticed that none of the staff talked to the children – not even to the children who should be able to speak because their problems were just physical; like a deformed foot or something similar. I realised that was why none of the children spoke. In fact when the staff saw us singing and talking to the children they would catch each others eyes and tap their foreheads as if we were mad.

The fortnight went by very quickly. The girls were returning to England; Anthea for Christmas and Susan for ever, as she was getting married.

Back at home I finished my arrangements. Everything went amazingly smoothly, I found tenants for Chapel Cottage, and handed over the running of the pottery to Ben and Elke who were now married and would be living in my cottage, and a month later I was ready to leave. I asked David and Shiela and a few close friends over for my 60th birthday supper, and the next day I went to London to stay overnight with my sister, Ann, before leaving for Romania.

Sadly, this felt a bit awkward as there was a silence about what I was doing – no argument, just silence. My two brothers Guy and Bruv were also silent about it. I was quite a lot younger than the others and had always looked up to them, and because I sensed their disapproval I had been too shy to explain why I was going.

There had always been a very strong loving closeness between the four of us, but it was not a closeness that bared its deepest feelings. The extent of our individual loves and pains remained private and were not aired. When real tragedy hit one of us, like the death of a child, or the breakup of a marriage, the outward reaction was as if nothing had happened, while at the same time enormous practical help was there, and at any time, if needed, there would be a bed, good food, amusing talk and laughter, but there was an unspoken sense that though deeper emotions were implicit they must never be explicit. These subtle undefined barriers were very strong and grew up I believe during the many separations and upheavals of our wartime childhoods, and though it would be impossible to actually say "I love you" it was there in the teasing insults and occasional hugs.

I wondered why they all disapproved, I had a feeling that they were suspicious of my motives; perhaps they felt I had 'got God' because my children were now grown up and it would sort of fill the gap. Maybe they thought that now I was trying to be a 'do gooder,' I knew that Bruv had quite an antipathy towards missionaries – he really hated them, as he hated people who went to other countries interfering and thinking that they knew best. Perhaps the others felt the same.

I did understand why they might feel this way, earlier I also had had to struggle with doubts when I wondered whether I was kidding myself in thinking that God was directing me – looked at coolly it seemed unlikely – perhaps it was my ego – was I being self-important to think that I could make any difference when there was so much suffering? How could I even touch the edge of it.....?

Then, at that time I heard a story:

"A man out walking came to a wide beach. The tide was far out and he saw that the beach was covered with hundreds of starfish stranded by the falling tide. Then he saw that there was a boy standing near the shore who was picking up starfish and throwing them into the sea. The man went up to him and said "Why bother, There are so many what difference will that make?" and the boy just picked up another starfish and as he threw it into the sea he said "It makes a difference to *that* one."

When I heard this I had felt the same reaction as when I had first read "feed my lambs", a shiver that had made all my hairs stand on end.

On the plane the next day I thought about Ann, and even wrote her a note that I never sent. I was aware that if Ann – one of the warmest most generous of people – had been told that there was a child confined in her front room; tied hand and foot permanently, and had been like that for months, she would have rushed in and rescued it immediately, she would not have been able to get on with her life knowing it was still tied there. What difference if the child is in Romania? How does distance alter their suffering? It is all the same.

Also on the flight I rather reluctantly read an article in the Readers Digest that someone had thought I should read. It was about a lady called Beverly Peberdy who went to Romania and met the Mother Teresa Sisters and eventually adopted a boy. She had gone to a different area than the one I was going to, and had worked in a different sort of set- up, but I was interested when she said how the contact with the sisters moved her and she had become a Christian. I never read the article again, but for some reason I remembered her name, and I was to come across it again later.

BRAILA

CHAPTER FOUR

I was surprised to be met in Bucharest Airport by Anthea and a young Romanian man called Ionel who I had met briefly in November. They told me that they were now engaged and that Ionel would be moving in with us. They took the living room and once again I had the bedroom.

The days fell into a pattern. Every morning Ionel (who at 27 was a few years younger than Anthea) went off to his job in the shipyard and Anthea and I went into the orphanage. There we did what we could.

There were 44 children who had all come from other orphanages having failed the basic assessment. Some had severe problems, but so many others who had just had small physical defects originally, were now suffering from the effects of malnutrition, neglect and sensory deprivation. Since November some had died and three were failing.

After a few weeks I began to keep a diary – not every day – and to start with; when everything was new, it was a place to jot down my first impressions. But then gradually, as time went on it became a place to unload pain, and my struggles to make sense of things. I call it a diary but there was no regular pattern to it. Some days I would scribble pages as the mood took me. At other time just a few sentences as a thought struck me, and sometimes there were long gaps. It felt more like sharing my life with a close friend. I have included these jottings in this account because though they are rough, they have an immediacy that something remembered years later might not have.

"Romania 15th March

Sunday: I have been here six weeks now and I am gradually getting used to things. This country, just starting to emerge out of fifty years of Communism, is deeply financially depressed – even staples like bread and bus fares have risen nearly every week since I have been here: and it's not just financial, one gets the feeling that the people are also depressed – there is so little colour.

We are living in a 'bloc', one of the large square blocks of apartments built by the communists. They all look a bit as if they are falling to pieces as cracks appear and bits fall off and nothing is ever repaired. On the ground level there are holes that had gratings on once – you can see the broken edges, inside there is a drop into some sort of totally black basement. These are the front doors of the small lithe feral cats. Other areas around the blocs also have their claimants, a large gentle thin dog has a patch of pavement in the front, the skip for the rubbish houses a small furry yellow dog. Gradually, as one starts looking around one begins to notice the signs of this underworld of feral dogs. Over the years they have been losing their breed characteristics and seem to be turning into yellowish, rather hairy jackal – like dogs. They seem to live their lives completely independent of humans and are completely benign. Sometimes they run in packs, I have seen 14 together, but more usually in twos or threes. Twice in the morning I have seen one of them lying quietly on its side, with a stillness that a closer look shows is death. At night they bark, it seems like hundreds of voices, which strangely have not lost their old breed timbres, because some are high, some low – some baying, some yapping, all barking on and on...they don't keep me awake at all – I just register the sound whenever I wake up – which is curious because back at home I have tossed and turned unable to sleep because of the solitary yapping of a neighbour's dog.

Our flat is considered very luxurious, it is near the Danube and has a sort of balustrade between us and the next bloc. When we came on the 1st of February the central area had cars parked among high banks of dirty snow, and the roads and pavements were paved with hard packed black ice, very uneven. My shoes – deck shoes – were totally inadequate and I had to buy a pair of the thick clumpy leather boots, like all the Romanians wear in the winter, which felt safe, warm and surprisingly comfortable.

Anthea's car, an Arow, which is a box shaped jeep type four wheel drive, only works intermittently and seems to get some new problem each time it goes out.

Our apartment is a curious mixture of luxury and inefficiency. The floors of the hall, kitchen and bathroom are marble or ceramic tiles and the other two rooms are parquet – which is the luxurious part. Also hot water, gas and heating are provided, though the water has a mind of its own. In the bathroom the hot and cold in the bath both work, but the washbasin only has cold, the hot tap does not work, and the lavatory cistern has to be filled with water before it can be flushed as it is always empty. To wash up we need to collect water from the bath tap as the kitchen hot tap does not work. Every now and then the hot water turns off, and less often both hot and cold go, so we have bottles of water on standby just in case. Then during the summer the hot water goes off for a month while repairs to the system are carried out.

The heating of the apartment is very fierce. Old fashioned radiators of the kind found in old schools belt out heat and the air is very dry, clothes hung up after washing, even if they are dripping wet, are dry in a few hours.

Oddly enough – considering conditions at the orphanage, I am not unhappy at the moment, and everything is relative. It was a bit awkward when I first came because Anthea had just got engaged to Ionel and he had just moved in. I did feel rather in the way to start with and spent hours on my bed reading to give them space on their own, or going for solitary walks along the Danube or into town, and every weekend and most evenings they would go off to visit the hundreds of relatives and church members etc. But now I have got used to it and feel much more at home.

How quickly one becomes used to the general poverty of the place, noticing instead the things that stand out as a contrast to the general deprivation and drabness – a coca cola poster seems like something from another world – which of course it is.

On the way to the orphanage I am struck by the very rural aspects of this large dusty town. Lots of horses and carts, one day I saw two men burning straw on the pavement and a closer look showed the blackened shape of a dead pig having its bristles burnt off.

The patches of earth between the verge and the pavement are used like small allotments by the house/shack adjacent; some are planted with vines that are led up rickety poles over our heads and into the yards of the house. Others are just being dug, and sewed with probably some sort of veg. With just a little bit of string tied to sticks to keep the dogs and walkers off. I did have the thought that in England the emerging vegetables would never escape vandals.

I get the impression that fear makes the Romanians very law abiding.

We have noticed at the orphanage that there is a marked absence of any sign of initiative or individualism – floors are only mopped at the allotted time – never mind however much wee or worse is on them between times, or how the children crawl over it and spread it about. As with the changing of the children, this seems to be done only at set times, and only by the 'lowly' people. Nurses would not dream of doing it, and I have seen the two doctors and a nurse on one of their rare walks around poke at a child lying on his back, tied, with cold vomit all over his neck and chest and decide he has a chest infection then continue on, without making any moves to change him. We are not encouraged to do any changing, washing or caring for the children, but sometimes when no one is looking we will have to change a dripping child before we can play, cuddle or take it down to our playroom.

Our role is not really understood by the Romanian staff, We can come in and choose whichever child we feel is most in need of some comfort or stimulation. We bring up a few toys and choose one of the salons to concentrate on trying to get the children there untied, out of their cots or chairs etc. and playing with something. We are not meant to interfere with any of the working of the orphanage. Therefore we have to turn a blind eye when children are put on potties and left there in a row for over two and a half hours, even being fed at 12 still sitting on their potties, too cowed to move off. (These pots ironically were provided by the Aid For Romania)

The salons are completely bare except for cots and a central table with built in chairs. Children are sometimes tied into these chairs for hours on end. There are no playthings of any sort. Over the year the girls have provided posters and toys and cot mobiles strapped to each cot but invariably they disappear, so sadly we need to count out anything we bring up and take it back down with us, or it too will have vanished by next day.

Many of the children are very disturbed and bang their heads on the cot railings. The girls provided cot bumpers but these too have disappeared, so these children are tied tight – hands and feet outstretched like starfish all the time.

One of these is Alin, he is ten and weighs 24lbs (what my daughter weighed at ten months.) He was better in November, just wandering around like a lost soul, introverted but not self destructive except for his habit of regurgitating his food immediately after a meal – hence his skeletal thinness. But when I returned in February he had deteriorated terribly, his head was covered with bruises from head banging, his face scratched from his picking, so his hands are kept continually tied behind his back.

I asked to be able to feed him, which I began to do *very* slowly, giving him the mush of potato, carrots and water in a tin cup that is their meal. I was appalled when they told me to only give him half as he vomited. This thinking seemed stupid – half of that almost starvation diet would not be enough for survival even if he never vomited again. However no one seemed to notice that he vomited a small amount even easier than a full feed, therefore he was only getting a fraction. I feel he is so desperately unhappy but also deeply angry. He does the only thing he can, which is to hurt himself. Also I had a hunch that his only pleasure in his starving state was food, and the regurgitating was a way of prolonging the eating, as the feeding by the staff is done impatiently and very fast, all over in a bare few minutes.

I began to untie him and take him to a quieter place where I hoped by rocking and singing etc. to calm him down a bit until the meal time, then having got Dr Stefan's grudging permission to take over his lunch time feeding for a two weeks trial, I have been feeding him about six eights of his mush (because his stomach is very shrunken) and then I take him downstairs where we have a box of baby jars of fruit and cereal – these are quite delicious and I just dip a spoon in and let him suck it off. It takes altogether almost an hour to finally finish the meal in this way. Then I try to distract him in some way to stop the regurgitating – at first it was not always successful, but only once did the whole lot come back. I don't have long to distract him because all the children have to be in their cots between 1 and 4pm. But I have found that to wrap him up and take him around the yard seems to do the trick. Then I take him upstairs feeling like I'm betraying him, and he is tied into his cot.

Sometimes his face creases up in a weak grimace of pure misery and I find, even though he is still very withdrawn, that by placing my hands on either side of his face and then leaning over and whispering into his ears that I will be back tomorrow, and a few kisses seems to stop the crying.

They have confirmed that he has not vomited these meals at all, but are not interested why, and make no effort to change their own way of dealing with things, so I guess breakfast, supper and the weekends are still chaos.

I worry about what I am doing – am I prolonging his agony – without this meal he will eventually die – but what of his future? I realise that before, when I was holding Alin, I was praying for God to make me able to heal him, and I now feel that that was not right because I was wanting to be the one who healed Alin with God's help, and of course it is the other way around.

I must not decide what I want God to do I must tune in more to what God wants me to do. Easier said than done.

I guess Alin is bright, but he does not say a word and does not respond in any way to anything except the sight of food. Though now when I come to him to take him out of his cot, when he is untied he will stand up and hold up his arms to be picked out. I have to be very careful for the first half an hour as his urge to bang his head is very strong, but after a quiet sit and rock and sing of a soothing repetitive song he seems to relax and gets heavier and heavier and his breathing becomes slower and deeper, even though he is not asleep.

He still insists on his hands being tied behind his back and is annoyed when I do it loosely as my instinct tells me. Apparently he had them always tied like this and it has become a habit now with him, his shoulder blades seem a bit distorted because of it, but after a cuddle he even relaxes a bit over this, and can even be put down while I attend to another child – though this is always risky as he could suddenly hit his head. The sad thing is that last November there was no self abuse. This is all a sign of his deterioration. Next Thursday I will weigh him again as my two weeks trial is up.

There is always the self doubt about whether we might not be making things worse for the children in the long run – their future is so bleak. At 16 they all get sent to an adult mental institution. Dr Stefan says matter of factly that most of them will die there in the first few months. He seems to think that this shows how much better his place is than theirs. He does not consider that it might be because the children have never been taught to feed themselves, learn any control of bladder and bowels, talk, or in a lot of cases even *walk*. Even strong children who can stand, run and jump in their cots, shuffle on their bottoms on the floor – they do not stand a chance. So we hope to make them a bit more able to cope, but it is a bit daunting with just two of us and nearly 50 children. When the self doubts come I seem again and again to come back to the idea that it is this minute that is important, and in a curious way in these times I have picked up the Bible and just random reading has repeatedly confirmed this, and I realise that for us and the children *now* is the only reality and our job is to make the *now* happier if we can. Simple in concept – hard in reality."

Chapter Five

Some weeks later....no date.

"Last night I read about Nehemiah who was angry that people, already poor, were made even more so by their own countrymen taking their assets and profits to pay interest on loans.

He pondered – and then approached the usurers and persuaded them not only to stop their exorbitant practices, but also to pay back what they had already taken.

I mentally picked out the word 'pondered' because that in some way seemed the key to the story. He was angry – but he did not just charge in ranting and raving – he pondered – this gave God a chance to help him, and then when he said something it really worked.

I picked it up because I am a lifelong crasher in, and one of the benefits of being in Romania is that for the first time I am beginning to ponder. It has happened naturally as I have so much more thinking time. And it's really amazing what a difference it can make.

In some things you realise that your first idea would not be appropriate, in other things you realise that your first impression was in fact wrong, or if not wrong, was at least biased, or you understand more why it was like it was.

But the best times are when what seemed just a passing thought is seen to have much more importance than you first realised, as in this instance – it started as an unconscious pick up of the word 'pondered' and after a night's sleep and some pondering on this word, came the sense that perhaps God is sometimes trying to tell us something, but we are usually so busy or so swept away by our own view of things that we don't hear even when He manages to get a word in edgewise.

Pondering can be a very creative time, a chance to allow thoughts and ideas to develop. The only difficulty that I can see is that it is not really something you can sit down and do – like "I will now sit down and ponder for half an hour." It is altogether more subtle than that. I have no choice in Romania. I have a lot of time when there is not much else to do. But when I get back – how can I keep from again getting swept up in a whirlwind of busyness? I will have to ponder on that one.

Sometimes on Fridays we take some of the more mobile children to the park, taking pushchairs and two Romanians, Arlena and Humitsa, to help, we have taxis and the children really love it. Starting by removing the ragged gowns they always wear and dressing them up in outdoor clothes – we have boxes of these donated – to the great joy of riding in a taxi and seeing something of the outside world, and then when we take them to the play area and show them the swings and slides they turn into just normal children. How quickly they overcome their fear of grass and uneven surfaces etc. and start calling to us to watch as they climb the steps of the slide and then shriek with joy as we catch them at the bottom. Last Friday there was a great moment when one boy, unused to the uneven surface, tripped and sat down backwards looking surprised, and suddenly another boy, Gheorgu, laughed. It was great as Gheorgu usually wanders around so disturbed that unless he is given something to hold in either hand he hits his head – this was the first time I have ever heard him laugh.

The joy of going to the park is that we seem to meld into a small group, and the children start to interact with each other, unlike the orphanage where each seems so isolated in their own lonely world.

I have gone into the main room where the mats on the floor are packed with the more mobile children with hardly room to move. The television is blaring and at least five members of the staff are sitting in a row gossiping and half watching the screen, taking no notice of the children except to shout and threaten them if they look like moving off the mats. I looked at every child, not one was looking at the television, which was showing an old Dallas like American serial with sub titles. At other times I have gone upstairs where children are crying, crawling over each other, tied to chairs etc and I have counted nine members of staff – one group looking at a film magazine, another group chatting and a couple filling in forms – it was as if they were blind and deaf, not one was paying any attention to the children.

It is the old conundrum; one feels they think they would run the orphanage very efficiently if it was not for the children being in the way. But it is saddening and frustrating because it is clear that it is not the number of staff that is the problem – there are plenty – it's that any motivation or interest are completely absent. I don't think they consider the children at all; even Dr Amelia will pick up a child by one arm as if it is a doll. They all do this – holding the child slightly away from themselves as if it is distasteful and thump the skinny little bare bodies down hard into the sinks, totally ignoring the weak cries of pain and distress.

The British have provided padded changing mats, these are beside each sink, but they are not used, the wet naked child is thumped down on a bit of torn sheet on the eating table in the middle of the room – there is a sort of hopelessness because so many things to make life easier for both the staff as well as the children have been sent out in the lorries and the results are so disappointing, because they are either accepted as being useful and so disappear, or are not accepted and so are not used. There seems to be a deep resistance to any change, as they seem to think the appalling conditions are acceptable.

Anthea said some visitors from the West have been shown around the place and go home to weep – shocked beyond belief by what they saw, i.e. Children whose legs have twisted completely out of shape, that at home with physiotherapy would have been walking – children with some physical problem like a cleft palate or twisted feet who were dumped in an orphanage at birth and so have never had the chance to develop their perfectly normal brains, so can't communicate let alone anything else. Some, a few perhaps, are mentally retarded, and these I feel are the lucky ones, as it is the bright child trapped in this lonely prison that I ache for.

A thought: I find looking back, even over quite a short period it becomes clear that God's perspective takes in the past, present and future.

The puzzling thing is that though He is the creator and can obviously 'do' anything and everything – He still seems to want our work and prayers in order to relieve suffering. In some ways this is a great honour that we are asked to work *with* God but also there is a fear of ones inability to do what is needed. The way to cope with this inadequacy is prayer, and so one gets to the curious situation of asking God to give you what is needed – to know what you must do – to do what God wants. In other words; a prayer that goes something like:

Help me God to pray so that you will tell me, and I will hear what I have to do in order to do what you want me to – and then help me to do it". Put like this it becomes clear that it all has to come from God.

The initial prayers need His help
The hearing needs His help.
The understanding needs His help.
The doing needs His help

Monday March17th

The willows are coming out along the Danube. Walking through the market I saw small piles of nettles for sale – little bundles wrapped around with cotton with half a carrot – some white vegetable (celeriac?) and a sprig of herbs. No more of the soft new salad lettuces, the two I bought were very insubstantial, just damp tasteless leaves without any substance, but they were the only veg apart from the old battered carrots and onions. On the river tugs push barges heaped high with coal, an amazing amount. Like railways, where I saw a freight train going at little over walking speed with forty coaches. Most freight seems to go this way.

Thursday.

On Tuesday we went to Bucharest to collect Fanica's and Corina's shoes from someone arriving from England. We both felt a bit of an anti climax as another car had also come so it was all over in five minutes and I think we had both been secretly looking forward to meeting another English person. I have not yet met anyone from the West.

In my reading one thing strikes me. We were told to love our neighbours – love our brothers – we weren't told to love them 'if they were good' we were just told to love them – whatever.

Why then do we doubt God's love for us? Why think he would not do what he tells us to do, which is to love without conditions?

I believe that whatever we do we are still loved, but if we choose to live without reference to God we grow unable to feel this love or be helped by it, and become cut off from God with the resultant confusion, unhappiness and stress.

I don't believe that God cuts *us* out; it is we who have the freedom to cut God out.

CHAPTER SIX

28th March.

Rather a gap since last writing, feeling a bit despondent at the atmosphere in the orphanage as Dr Stefan seems very negative and almost pleased to point out that Alin has been sick.

There was a bit of a rumpus on Monday. It went like this, after taking an hour to slowly feed Alin, (for some time I have been bringing in minced food from home to supplement his orphanage meal), but there is the awkward time when I have just finished when he is liable to regurgitate his meal. He is too deeply depressed to be distracted by any of the usual methods –books – toys etc. but we found a walk around the yard seemed to take his mind off food for a while On Monday I felt he was a bit tense as he was so set back by the weekend, and so hastily we put on an anorak with a hood, a jersey a second pair of trainer pants and socks – but – and here comes the crunch – no woolly hat, just pulling up the hood as I went out.

It was a sunny, cool, spring day, I did not even have a jersey on myself, just a T shirt, as I walked Alin around in my arms. Suddenly Dr Stefan burst indignantly out of the orphanage, he had seen us from his window and ordered us in, briskly pointing to the bit of leg showing between the sock and the rucked up pants.

In the playroom a small row erupted. Anthea indignantly defending my action, saying loyally that Alin would now be dead if it wasn't for me, and also we pointed out that when I had gone to get Alin at 11.30 he was lying in a cold wet bed with his hands tied tightly to the bars and cold sick from breakfast all over his chest – rather more likely to give him pneumonia in our opinion than being carried around a sunny yard for a few minutes wrapped in an anorak.

This did not go down at all well and we were told that I was too old to remember how to bring up children and Anthea had not had any children and so would not know – whereas he had two boys and would know best. We then pointed out that Alin had gained half a kilo since I had been feeding him. Again a negative reaction,

"Had I got the paper to prove it?" I had, and luckily not signed by me, but by some strange sort of foresight that I could not quite justify at the time, I had got Alena, the Romanian educator to weigh him with me and also to sign the paper. So then Dr Stefan said it must be the same time of day and in the same clothes, and we pointed out that it was, and anyway the children always had the same clothes, a hospital type gown open at the back and tied with ties and ragged trainer type pants. But what I was realising was that he did not care if Alin was gaining weight or not, what he wanted to do was to catch us out. On reflection one of the saddest things was his remark – with some truth – that these children were not used to being outside so it is dangerous for them. So sad, because these children are not there because of any physical illness, – physically they could be perfectly normal children. They are classified as being mentally retarded, and there again in a lot of cases this is nonsense. Ionel with his cleft palate, Fanica and Corina with their turned over feet, the AIDS children, and I am sure many more had perfectly normal brains initially.

What saddened me was though he was right in a sort of way, it was so unnecessary. At the Chernovoda Hospice, run by English volunteers, all the children are physically ill with AIDS but there the rooms were fresh and airy with open windows, and they wear proper clothes and play outside all the time. Even Dr Stefan, when Anthea and Susan once took him there, remarked that they looked like 'well' children, but somehow he won't make the necessary adjustment to compare that with his awful airless hot steamy place where what could be physically well children are continually going off to hospital with pneumonia.

We realise that the panic about the danger of draughts and fresh air, and putting on layers of clothes to go out whatever the actual day's temperature, is a deeply ingrained Romanian obsession. But feel despondent that Dr Stefan, having seen how rosy happy and bouncy the children are at the Chernovoda hospice and even remarked about it in wonder; he still does not alter his set views one jot. He is a doctor but claims that cerebral palsy is caused by the mother going out in the sun, and other weird old wives' tales.

Thankfully he did not come in on Tuesday and Wednesday – he was briefly in on Thursday when he coldly pointed out that Alin was still being sick, and then on Friday almost the last shred of my respect for him went.

It was a warm, still sunny day – really lovely – and it was the going to the park day. The children were very excited and were dressed ready in an assorted layer of clothes and warm jerseys but not the smart new anoraks (brought from England) because they were locked upstairs and could not be used because the lady with the key was not on duty. So the trip was cancelled by Dr Stefan. The excuse being that they did not have the right clothes. By then the two taxis I had ordered were waiting outside.

We were told they could play in the yard which is little more than a fenced area of rubble, rusty pipes and concrete. I asked ironically if the air was different in the yard than in the park, but in retrospect it was unwise. I paid off the taxis and tried to control my anger and disappointment.

Anthea was not there as she and Ionel were due to go to Bucharest that day in the jeep, but it was cancelled and so they turned up at this point and Anthea went up to try to persuade Dr Stefan to change his mind. She succeeded and we all piled into the Arow and went off. His justification for changing his mind was that with the Arow we could come back if it got cold, but I had a sneaking feeling that he is very 'off' me, but still wishes to keep in Anthea's good books. It can't really be about the clothes because they were completely bundled up, but then he said to Anthea that it was Alena's wish not to go as the children did not look so smart. Alena seemed rather vague about it all so I don't really know what it was all about. What I do feel though is that Dr Stefan is extremely negative in reality while trying to seem on our side on the surface and the pretence is really starting to slip.

Unfortunately after 8 weeks here I am really beginning to dislike the Romanians, as incident after incident increasingly makes me despise them. These incidents are many and varied so I won't go into a negative recital of them, but there are too many to ignore the gradual build up of a real dislike – I wish it were not so, it would be so much easier to see them as a lovely people who have been oppressed – but sadly I can't.

The nice thing is that the thing I had imagined might be difficult was the children. With their rotten teeth and smelly bodies and breath, their lack of any toilet training or nappies, with the inevitable mess. Their shaven heads and sores and the way they cling and clamour for attention and their disturbed self abusive behaviour. All these things made me feel that I might find myself having to steel myself to handle and love them in the close personal way that is essential. But on the contrary I suddenly realised that they are the best thing about my life here because they are so innocent and lovable they seem like a breath of fresh air compared to the adults.

Yesterday we drove to Sinaia. My first trip away from Braila except for the day in Bucharest. It was in the mountains, a monastery and an amazing Bavarian type palace built in the end of the last century. Inside it was over the top kitsch, every surface carved and decorated – rooms ornate and oppressive and windows of stained glass seemingly closed to the lovely views with such thick bottle glass that you could not see through. It was a happy day, sunny in the morning and snow showers in the afternoon, though a long three and a half hours in the unheated Arow. I offered to treat us to a restaurant lunch and we all had soup and a main course and it came to 4.500. approx £4.50. The diesel for the car has risen from 600l a litre to 2000 plus since December.

Oh how negative this diary is. Perhaps that's its purpose.

Later

One lovely thing happened earlier this week. I had had a phone call from [my sister] Ann, very late at night with the two hours difference, and felt very sad after it because we are not getting through to each other in a straight way any more. I'm not sure what is the problem exactly, and we both pretend it is not there – but it is . I found I could not sleep and it worried me on and off all night. I prayed to be able to resolve it, and later felt that it might be a good idea to write to Ann as I have not done so yet.

I mentioned that the call rather saddened me – she had talked a lot about poor [aunt] Tunta who seems to be failing and Ann is helping her. I feel sorry for Ann who is in the middle of what must be a very stressful period of selling her home, where she has been for 40 years, and buying the new house, and the resultant move and sorting out of furniture etc. must loom, so maybe that is part of the trouble – also I feel that she does not understand why I am here and thinks I must have some complicated reason, as she mentioned guilt.

Anyway the letter turned out to be very long as I told her all about our work at the orphanage and life here as honestly as I could and by the end was able to lighten up a little.

Anthea and Ionel were out and I went into the sitting room to get the glue to stick on the stamps (essential with Romanian stamps) and put the letter down on the ironing board while I got the glue from the cupboard. Then I took the stamps and glue and letter to the sofa to stick them on only to find that instead of picking up the letter from the ironing board I had Anthea's bible in my hand. I looked at it, puzzled, and then wondered whether it was just a rather extraordinary absent minded action on my part or whether I was meant to look at the bible. So again I did Granny's thing and let it fall open. The first two tries it opened at places where Anthea had put cards, so I closed it again and the third time looked closely at it and opened it very slowly so the pages just eased away from each other and saw that it was opening at the end where there were no bookmarks so I let it open fully, and again, like before, I read where my eye first fell.

It was 1 John. Chapter 4. Verse16 to the end, and it was all about love. It was really wonderful, and ended with the advice that one must love one's brother for you could not love God who you don't know if you don't love your brother who you do – for 'brother' I read sister. The whole passage was so wonderful and there were the words "God is love" that had come into my head out of the blue so many years before and I had never known where it came from in the Bible. It confirmed that the only thing that matters is the love we feel for each other, this is such a blessing that small differences are so petty compared with that.

Peter Kidd sent me Corrie Ten Boom's 'The Hiding Place' which I am reading and makes my small work here pale into insignificance compared to what she had to do: very salutary but also inspiring.

It made me see that we are the tools of God. We must not waste this life we have been given by remaining in the tool box. You might be a power drill, I might be a tack, but God needs all his tools not just power drills. He needs tacks and nails and hammers and chisels, even sandpaper. I don't think we decide what we are . God decides for us what he needs us for.

I personally don't think God categorises his tools either in the "hammers are better than nails" sort of way. Both are essential to get the job done. But it is essential that we be wholehearted in whatever we are asked to do. And we must not forget that we are HIS tools (the hammer must not go around knocking at any old nails that it sees because it does not like the way they stick up) Sometimes we are directed in a way that seems a bit surprising or hopeless, but we can't see the whole picture. God can. If we obey then perhaps, much later, we will see the complete picture and why we needed to do that particular thing at that particular time.

I sense that if we don't do what we are asked for various reasons, we are never told what might have been if we had obeyed- though I wonder if there is not a sense of loss.

I still feel that there are truths that I can only sense at the moment, and probably will never be able to fully grasp them. But this sense of the greatness of God, even if not really understood is very real. This is very exciting as it makes the ordinary extraordinary and the familiar profound.

There is a link up with my learning here so I do not feel alone – like I found something in 1 John by chance and a bit later reading Nicky Gumble re found it – the same passage. Or again reading Nicky Gumble where he mentions a text, and going to look up the text I find it on the page where I had my bookmark (1264 pages in my bible) these are the more obvious examples, but there are so many subtle ones, the net result of all this seems to be telling me I am not alone. I am so helped in this voyage of exploration.

Sunday March 30th

Today is Easter day at home – my little [balcony] garden has flowered today. Little blue flowers like tiny hyacinths, just two on every stalk. What I forgot to say about our trip yesterday to Sinaia was how lovely it was walking down the cobbled track – snowy underfoot but we had good boots, with the gentle spring snowflakes drifting down. And the air was such a joy, so clear and fresh and crisp we really appreciated it after Braila's polluted atmosphere. I bought some little old fashioned wooden toys for Joel and Tom [grandsons] at a craft stall – pecking chickens, a snake in a box and animals that move when you push the bottom of their stand up, and some dear little wooden scoops to use for salt containers in the pottery. They only cost about 10 English pence each, though by Romanian standards much more. I had a happy daydream about the pottery on the drive home imagining myself making the salt containers and wondering whether to do them tin glaze with blue or terracotta – they would make lovely gifts with the tiny wooden scoops.

CHAPTER SEVEN

Wednesday 2 April

This week has been a mixture of chaos and encouraging signs – the best thing was when I went in on Monday there was the usual rush of children clinging onto me, and hovering behind them was the anxious face of Alin – up – not tied into his cot. And he has stayed up all this week, no longer banging his head on the floor, or in fact any hard surface, and better still most of the time with his hands not tied behind his back. So today I was able to help the other children while keeping an eye on Alin. I brought some warm water with a spot of honey and intended to give him a few spoonfuls every now and then during the morning, not enough for him to bring up but have an accumulative effect on his dehydration.

Early last week I had changed my previous routine of giving him some nice food just before his orphanage lunch, as I thought that if I gave him this directly I came it might help the terribly empty stomach to have little and often rather than a bigger lunch. But of course he has no idea of time and so after that early feed was looking about for his orphanage feed and got upset and was sick. So now we are back to the original routine and I am sure his tummy is changing shape. It was so difficult spending such care and time over feeding him and not knowing for sure whether the food stayed down. But now I have begun to know if it is ok (even though we have to leave the orphanage once the children were all confined to cots), because if he was sick after we left the staff always told me next day with a sort gloating satisfaction. It saddened me that they seemed to see this as some sort of triumph.

This week he is gradually becoming less listless. He watches what is going on, seems to need me being around, but now he is on his feet he no longer needs continual holding and wanders off from time to time.

I do notice when I feed him, however, he snuggles close in a very familiar way, rather as if over these weeks we have grown used to the feel of each other. I still have to keep quite an eye on him because he grabbed some soap and hid it in the back of his trousers [to eat later] and then a bit later I saw him reach to the sink where there was a pot of detergent powder and put some in his mouth and luckily I saw and was able to wash it out of his mouth, oddly enough he seemed to quite enjoy this, (I remember last November finding him scooping handfuls of nappy rash cream into his mouth) then later when I was feeding him I found a little piece of soap hidden in his trouser leg and felt awfully mean when I took it away. But in a way all this is an encouraging sign that he is coming to life again, and I remember him as he was five weeks ago, lying spread-eagled, tied hand and foot, eyes sunk deep in their sockets and his whole body so emaciated and weak. But the most disturbing thing was the way he seemed to have completely given up – not responding to anything – eyes completely dead of any expression. Now he again seems to be looking out of them.

12th April

This seems such a weird country. I feel living here is like swimming in a sea where though the surface is warmer, you are conscious that some way below the surface there is a dark strong current that would sweep anyone away who puts a foot down. Inflation is still rampant. Petrol was 600 lei per litre in December. Two weeks ago it was 2,500 lei per litre. Stamps here are a different price every time I buy them. When I first came they were 1600l for a letter home yesterday it has risen to 6500l, hardly room to get them all on the envelope.

The Post Office is curious, officially the town's main P.O. After going through the usual metal barred and broken glass door, you find yourself in a vast marble hall; once grand with marble counters – now dirty and dingy with hardly any lighting and no customers usually. A clerk is hand stamping, there seems no filing system, just one small battered metal cabinet, but mostly brown cardboard folders piled haphazardly on a small table. To collect a letter you hand them the slip left in your letter box at the apartment, and there it is – among the small pile on the counter, unfiled. Any package, even a newspaper or paperback book had 6 different rubber stamps on it and three different signatures. Even ordinary letters are stamped three times in Romanian before one gets them, and a parcel is even more complicated . They must be collected across the town, by the station, between 8 and 1300 hours. As always in Romania, the office has no cupboards, just untidy piles of folders which, as always in any office seem to have to be flipped through to find the necessary form to sign. Fee paid, and then off he goes to get your parcel, which must then be opened, contents examined and remarked upon, and off we go. As Anthea gets food parcels almost every fortnight we are on first name terms.

I always get the impression that there is hardly any mail by Western standards. The girl who delivers our letters has no mail bag but just a small bundle of letters in her hand. Any letter whether delivered to our door, or collected from the post office if we are out, has to be signed for opposite where someone has written our name and address in copperplate writing. In fact almost everything in Romania needs forms signed and rubber stamped. These forms are invariably on paper very reminiscent of unbleached lavatory paper – coarse and absorbent.

The people cling to bureaucracy with a sort of desperate seriousness. We are getting very familiar with the police station as the extension of our visas took many trips, and meant hours of waiting. Then two policemen turned up at the flat to say we must go down next day for yet another session for some sort of identity card – more queuing and more passport photographs and being sent across town for some sort of tax to be paid, then back with the receipt to the police department – as usual no filing system, brown folders on desk shuffled through until he finally finds what he wants, and then in a couple of weeks another visit and queue etc. to pick up the necessary cards. There is no system of cheques, everything is cash and with inflation this means wads of money. All the small details of life – like paying for phone – electricity – etc. mean a trip to the appropriate office – queue, present bill, wait until piles of paper heaped on a desk have been searched through – pay – then off to another office to get an itemised account – this time a computer readout, a very rare thing, but this is only available about a week after the bill has been paid. As usual it is found eventually among what looks like a random pile of other papers on someone's desk. Always one must have the correct papers, correctly signed, for anything to go ahead. Everything is done very slowly and ponderously as if there is not enough work to fill the day – so all work must be done *very* slowly – despite the queues.

Here so much manpower is used – teams of people sweeping the streets and pavements with besom brooms, then leaving little piles of dust etc. to be collected by someone else who usually arrives when most of the little piles have been blown away – no one seems to mind. Like all jobs it does not seem to matter how badly they are done as long as you are seen doing something, it's like seeing everything in slow motion. The gardeners who attend to the rose beds in the boulevard are a team of women who poke around with old spades in a desultory fashion, and in the summer the grass is cut with sickles, and in the usual Romanian way, there are two people for every job, one to do it and another to stand beside him watching.

The people seem so very depressed – the inflation must be one explanation, bread goes up steadily – but it must be a lot deeper than that – I hunger for an open cheerful face. Beggars are everywhere, these are *real* beggars – aged people – people without limbs or with limbs so distorted you can hardly believe it, until you remember the children at the orphanage whose limbs are gradually twisting permanently stiffly out of shape due to lack of physiotherapy. Sometimes it's like having landed in a Breughel painting as stumps are thrust in your face as you queue for tickets. The only provision for one legged people are old fashioned wooden crutches or a wooden leg.

Our neighbour in the next apartment died two weeks ago and again one becomes aware of the absence of modern life, no undertakers, the dead have to be dealt with by their family or friends. As these apartments are heated from a central source you cannot turn the heating off and the poor frantic widow came to get our help to get him out of the apartment after a few days. It meant carrying the coffin down flights of stairs and into our jeep. They were unable to shut the back door, which perhaps in the circumstances was a good thing. A neighbour had tried to inject the body with formaldehyde but did not have enough so it had not worked. Anthea went to the funeral next day and said it was *very* unpleasant as the coffin, in the usual way, was open. I cowardly used the excuse that I had never met the man to keep well out of the way.

Yesterday, as you can probably gather, was a bad day, a really strong case of "I hate this awful country". However, blossom is starting to show buds in the yards of the little houses, and I do like the way each house turns the small patch of earth around it into a smallholding. People live this rural way – perhaps it's the only way they survive, I understand why the shops are so bleak, bare and under stocked because people don't really use them. Everywhere are horses and carts with bulging sacks – people with chickens with their legs tied and their poor heads craning as they are carried upside down – pigs – and people with small metal handcarts pushing more of the bulging sacks. We learn from Ionel that these are sacks of corn being taken to be milled into flour. Obviously people bake their bread as there are piles of yeast for sale on the market stalls. Then there are sacks of beans etc and also in the market great slabs of white tasteless cheese. It is crumbly and wet. And I believe Polenta [called mamaliga here,] is eaten a lot. Our Western type of shopping and eating is very rare.

No date

Long break since writing last – I became more aware that these three months have been necessary for me in my search for God. First the work in the orphanage which needs compassion which has to be kept alive and not blunted by the hourly, daily, constant sight and sound of the children's suffering. The staff are indifferent as they consider the children stupid as they have been classified 'mentally handicapped' and use the age old human excuse "they can't feel anything." However suffering is suffering whatever the mental state of the sufferer – and of course the classification of the children is patent nonsense, so many we can see are as potentially bright as any child – just undeveloped having being confined all their lives to their cots.

To face the reality, even for a moment, of the desperation of these children's lives and future is so shocking that one has to focus on the moment only – the moment of giving Fanica and Corina walking practice – seeing Gheorgu has something in his hands so he does not hit his head – going down the rows of cots [often with four children to a cot] touching, smiling, and talking to each one and enjoying the lovely smiles that one sometimes gets in return. Though this is not always easy, with Fanica, Corina, Georgu and Alin all clamouring for attention. And then finally at the end of the morning, feeding Alin.

There is a real struggle not to react too negatively to the staff – not to care as you carry a child past three watching staff and hear their sniggering laughs as you walk by. Their complete power over the children gives them opportunities for daily cruelties. Like someone walking past Vasile, who has AIDS and slapping him across the face, and when we expressed our dismay, shrugged, and said "He can't feel it." The larger cruelties caused by their laziness and indifference are something they do not seem aware of, lulled by the knowledge that this is the way that things are done. There is such a resistance to any change.

Be thankful for the few members of staff, usually the more lowly cleaners, who treat the children kindly and smile warmly at us. Sometimes, as happened this morning, a child, flooded with tears runs up to you as you arrive and clings, sobbing. You can't know the cause but just try to comfort as well as you can. The Romanian staff are sitting around indifferent, and we notice that it is always to us that the children come, never to them."

Here the diary stopped for a long while.

CHAPTER EIGHT

I was getting to know the other children. Each day, after spending some time with the children in any one of the four salons, we would choose a few to take down to our little playroom where we were able to give them more individual attention. There they were totally happy – like Adrienne, a dear child who had stiff twisted legs and so lay permanently on her back. She so loved being picked up and carried around that she laughs when you first pick her out of her cot. When I put her in the ball pool with various toys she would pick them all up and play with them so beautifully that I was sure that she was mentally bright. Then there was Paula who had very slight cerebral palsy and adored anything that glittered or is beautiful. I made her a hair slide with a biro top, and earrings out of sellotape and shiny paper. She was thrilled to find a mirror and looked and looked. Her poor hair was matted and dirty and her clothes were rags, but she only saw what she wanted to see which was beautiful. Sometimes we sat together on the floor and opened one of the shoeboxes that was full of little things had been sent by some little girl in England, and slowly took the things out– it was like a Christmas stocking – everything turned over an looked at with wonder, and then finally all put back in the box until next time.

Another one was Mihai, frustrated because he can't talk, and very active with a short attention span, but he is one of the most loving of children. And Monel, who was a survivor, he was very dark and strong and well built, the staff called him 'gypsy' in a derogative way. He would take no notice while they screamed at him. He had got into the habit of diving into our playroom whenever he could get away, and grabbing at some toy and frantically playing with it for the few seconds before a member of staff roared in and dragged him away. We began to suspect he was deaf and so brought him in – to his great joy, and gave him the hooter off the little bicycle which he held close to his ear while he hooted it loudly, he also began banging a xylophone with terrific concentration, again with his head very close to the keys.

And then there was Gheorgu, At first I had found him a very ugly child with his slight squint, beaky nose and rotten teeth, but he became a great favourite and was a great hugger. He had no concentration and liked to take off my shoes and gently pinch my legs all over. He spent a lot of his time sitting on the floor with his legs straight forward rocking his body to and fro, and needed to have some little toy put immediately into both of his hands directly he was untied to stop him hitting his head..

About this time a good thing happened. My brother Guy, who lived in Italy got in touch by fax. I have always been close to Guy, but because he had lived for most of his life abroad I did not see him often, and it was so good to hear from him, it seemed in an unspoken way he was offering support. One day, when I was upset and frustrated about things, I had written rather a desperate fax where, instead of being bright and cheerful I told it as it was. I got an immediate and concerned reply and it helped me so much to know that he was there, and was supportive that I did not need to unload my frustrations again.

A new lady doctor had arrived to help Dr Stefan, and at first we were encouraged but soon hope died as it became clear that she, like Dr Stefan, did not like having any contact with the children. Once when I tried discussing Alin's progress with her she just told me to move as I was blocking her view of the television.

Every afternoon when we left, I walked slowly home visiting the market to get something for supper, and then back to the flat. The first thing would be to change and wash off the orphanage smells, and then have a short sleep, and then it was my time to read. I seemed to have an insatiable appetite to read the bible that Ben and Elke had given me when I left, and the Christian books that I had brought with me.

A real asset was the book of the Alpha Course. I had gone to the first two sessions before I left home, but now I was able to study the text. It was so easy to read because Nicky Gumble was a natural storyteller and had a great sense of humour, and explained in a very straight forward way the basic principles of Christanity. It was my A B C as a new Christian. I had also brought some lighter books, but found myself ignoring them because they did not give me the sort of spiritual support that I needed at that time.

Anthea and Ionel understandably spent all their free time together. (Ionel had taken over the girl's jeep, and in the Romanian way he decided that only he should drive it: I noticed you did not see many women drivers) So I had many hours alone, which was strange after my busy life up until then, but I found that after a morning in the orphanage I loved this quiet recovery time.

I enjoyed taking over the shopping and cooking. Every week I drew out the equivalent of 20 pounds from the bank; (a long drawn out process,) which covered the rent and all our food. (Anthea previously seemed to live on packets of ready-made dried meals that her mother sent out to her.) There were no shops as we know them, sometimes there was something that looked like a shop but with rows of empty shelves – once I was delighted to see some large jars of pallid bottled peas – it had seemed so long since we had had any vegetables – but when I tried to buy one I was not allowed because I did not have an empty jar to exchange.

I spent quite a bit of time exploring and finding odd little markets and places where I could buy food. In the very early spring elderly ladies would sit at market stalls with nothing for sale but some neat little piles of nettle tops, they were the only fresh green thing I had seen for weeks. and when I bought a pile it would be scooped up in her bare hands. Nettles were used by the Romanians to add to their soups which were made with litres of water and some bottled vegetables. These soups were so thin that the bits of red pepper looked like tiny goldfish in an aquarium. The other winter staple was cabbages preserved in deep wooden barrels. These cabbages were very wet, and were piled up on stalls looking like boiled babies heads. I never tried them but supposed they would be like sauerkraut.

I enjoyed the challenge of finding food. I loved the crumbly feta-like cheese. And potatoes were also around, though they were very unattractive to western eyes, being wizened and sprouting and sometimes rotten: The smell of rotten potatoes was unbelievable, but you could always cut out the bad bits. But the best thing of all was called Babosh bought from roadside stalls. They were flattish rounds of dough – rather like a discus, that were removed from the hot fat and slapped to and fro on a plate of coarse sugar and then wrapped in paper and handed to you. They were cheap and filling and unbelievably delicious. You could also buy chickens in the market which were quite skinny and needed a bit longer cooking but were full of flavour.

One of the things I began to notice was a sense that everyone was frightened. The feeling of fear was palpable. People avoided your eyes and there were no smiles, and if I smiled it was not returned. I realised that though the country was no longer officially Communist, Braila, which was near the Soviet border in the far East of Romania, still retained the same people in power and the same police – the Securite – which I was told had been the most oppressive in the Soviet Bloc, with more people denounced to the Securite and more 'disappearances' than in any other communist country. This might explain that undercurrent of fear. Even though I dressed drably and tried to look inconspicuous I was recognised as a foreigner and people seemed frightened to even look at me. I was once followed for half an hour by a man calling out "C.I.A."

On another occasion I was approached on the way home from work by a man dressed almost in rags. He was a cultured man and spoke perfect English and told me in an urgent whisper that he was a professor, but because he had criticised the government he had lost his job and they had tried to kill him. He had managed to avoid it so far but said they would get him in the end. I suggested that now Romania was no longer communist it would be different but he laughed bitterly and just shook his head.

I was reading the New Testament for the first time and I began to see things in a new light. Before I became a Christian my image of Jesus was of a nice man surrounded by children and lambs and blue birds etc. – A nursery school sort of image of 'gentle Jesus meek and mild,' verging on the soppy. This was a time of seeing things in a different way and it was very exciting. I wrote it down as I had began to realise how much I had not understood.

"Somehow here the bible seems much more contemporary, it's not like a story that happened a long time ago, I realise that the *human* reasons that Christ was crucified was because he offended people's ideas about what should or should not be said or done. There seem to me to be parallels between the society that Christ was born into and the society of Romania, in that both were struggling under a very dominant yoke. In Christ's time it was the Roman occupation and in Romania it was communism. These very oppressive ruling forces in both cases stifled individualism – the religious hierarchy became rigid and rule bound and very linked with the ruling faction. Christ was crucified because he said and did things that deeply offended the code of his day. He showed them up as hypocrites, he cut across everything that they felt should or should not be done. He broke the rules.

Both societies lacked compassion for individuals. They were so out of touch with compassion that when Christ healed a lame man on the Sabbath they were more concerned that he told the man to pick up his mat than that after a lifetime of lameness the man could now walk. To pick up a mat on a Sabbath broke the rules – the rules had become all important.

I find Romania a very difficult country because here the rules are also all important. There is very little compassion for the individual. Fear has made people rigidly conformist. Those who could or would not conform were made to suffer for it – the more the lack of conformity the more the suffering, even unto death.

This was the same in both societies, and because of it terrible individual cruelties were done that no one seemed to notice or care about. Some of these cruelties are not intentional as such but come about by the people's inability to question the system.

Christ showed this for what it was. He did not just say it was wrong, he healed and cared about the actual people. They were so often people that the oppressive society considered were useless, the vulnerable and despised.

It seems that in Christ's time – like ours – the people were desperate for what he had to show them. They must have felt that all was not right the way it was, they followed him in thousands. However they did not stay with him. They weren't there protesting when he was crucified.

Perhaps fear was the reason. I think I understand a bit more how this could have happened. Fear is very real and it takes great courage to step outside the boundaries.

He said "We *must* love" What he said and did becomes very appropriate to Romania - I feel it's as if he knows Romania - what he says is what needs to be done. These parallels make the hundreds of years difference fall away, (even literally - today I saw a boy wandering along the railway track with a herd of goats while they grazed the new grass by the side of the track. So now the New Testament has become an actual working hand book. I am amazed, and for the first time really sense the incredible bravery in doing what he did: caring for the despised, his insistence on love, how odd that must have seemed.

In our society the word 'love' has been debased. "I love ice cream.....that pop group.....and so on... endlessly. We have forgotten how alternative it must have been in Christ's time. The love he talked about was so different - so wildly courageous, like swimming against a strong current. Until I went out to Romania I did not have a clue how brave Christ's teaching was.

Though he knew he was the Son of God, I don't believe he was in a privileged position that shielded him from fear and dread. He was not like Batman or Superman, he was very human, it is clear he was just as liable as we are to these things, like us he had to cope with them."

Because I heard the stories of Christ's teaching before I could begin to understand them, I tended to shrug them off, unaffected by them because of their familiarity. I failed to grasp that in his time they were not familiar at all. What he said was was almost unthinkably alternative to the current ways of thought. I find it a great help to realise this."

Suddenly, reading Jesus' words, and understanding more the nature of the people he was talking to, I was overwhelmed at the bravery of his message. From the start he knew, both spiritually, and as a man, that this would lead inevitably to just one conclusion. He had just three years to change the whole world.

Wherever he said 'the many' I felt a rush of excitement – we were the many –he meant us! It was so extraordinary. And if he meant us then he must mean us now. So he was here with us – *now*. And he would understand Romania and the oppression and the cruelty, and he loved these helpless children. That was when I began to personally love Jesus.

CHAPTER NINE

For a short while we were lucky enough to find a speech therapist and paid her to come and help the children learn to speak. She was married to a doctor and said they were very frightened as they were sure they would be purged. I never understood why. I liked her and she confirmed that many of the children could be taught to speak given time – sadly this did not happen as after a few weeks Dr Stefan told her to leave.

One day a curious thing happened. Off the main boulevard there was a cinema where they showed old American films with sub titles. One day we noticed that leaflets were being posted around advertising the free showing of a film about Jesus, and we found that it was organised by a Christian group who went all around Eastern Europe showing this film.

On the day it was due Anthea and Ionel could not go as they had some other plans, but filled with curiosity and anticipation I trotted off. I was expecting to see a crowd of people converging on the cinema, as a free film would be something very novel, but I was a bit disappointed to see no one. I thought that perhaps I had got the time wrong because as I approached the cinema I could see through the glass doors into the foyer and there were no people. Then I noticed that at the bottom of the windows there were the tops of small bobbing heads and as I entered I realised that I was the only adult and the foyer was packed with excited children. They were all the ragged street children and young beggars that we saw everywhere.

Then a pained manager opened a door and we all swarmed into the cinema, and the racket was tremendous as the excitement mounted. I was quite disappointed and a bit cross that not one other adult had taken up the offer. Then the film started and I realised that it was in English with no sub titles and my heart sank – the children would not understand a word, it seemed such a waste.

The film showed the story of Jesus' life told simply using only his words as spoken in the bible.

Gradually the hubbub died down as the children began to watch, and as the story unfolded they grew silent; all watching intently, even though they could not understand a word. Finally the film ended with Jesus' death and resurrection. There was a stunned silence and then pandemonium broke loose as the children clapped and cheered, it was a standing ovation. I was amazed by these homeless children who had so little comfort in their lives and yet here they were lit up by joy and clustering around a young man who had appeared who was asking their names and giving them leaflets about Jesus.

As I walked home I was ashamed of my previous disap-pointment – Jesus would not have been disappointed by this young scruffy audience – he would have loved them – just as it seemed they had loved him.

My first three months was nearly up, and sitting out on our little balcony I suddenly felt completely overwhelmed with dread at the thought that I must return after my break at home. It was very powerful and I was near tears, I was holding one of Nicky Gumble's books, ' A Life worth Living' and opened it on page 113 and as I read my heart was flooded with relief as the words spoke so directly to me, and once again I was shown that I was not alone. I was so moved by this break through that I immediately wrote a letter to Nicky Gumble telling him what a difference it had made to me.

Anthea and Ionel were planning to go to England for the month of August for their wedding. It would be for the last month of my second three month session here, and I felt I wanted to have someone else here with me. I did not want to be alone here. Judy, a friend of my sister's had said she would be interested in coming so I had written to her telling her about what to expect, but had had no reply. I resolved to contact her when I returned to England for a few weeks break.

In May I was back home again, and the joy of being with friends and family again completely absorbed me and though I knew I would have to contact Judy about her coming out to join me for the month of August I rather forgot to do it as I was so enjoying just being at home for this short while.

Then one day Ben had a telephone call from a young man called Peter Cleave who he had met briefly once. Peter was a very lively and enthusiastic Christian and said that God had told him three times that he must come and pray at Welcombe – he did not know why, but as Ben was the only person he knew in Welcombe could he come to us? Ben of course agreed and Sam decided to join us, then David and two other Christian friends of Ben's also invited themselves over so there was quite a group of us when Peter arrived. First everyone prayed at the house and then we walked down to the sea, then a bit more prayer and back home for a cup of tea.

Peter explained that he had to come that day as tomorrow he would be helping drive a truck of supplies to Romania, and Ben said "Mum's just back from Romania." And Peter said he knew someone who wanted to do the sort of work I was doing. I asked him to tell me who it was because I would be alone there for a month in August, then I remembered Judy and corrected myself, telling Peter that it was not necessary as I already had someone who had said they would come.

A few minutes later the phone started ringing and it was Judy to say briefly that she was sorry but she could not come. So I was able to turn to Peter and ask for the name of his contact. All he remembered was her name, Doreen Jones, and that she lived in Kilkhampton.

The next morning I looked up Joneses in the telephone directory and was a bit taken aback to see so many of them, but I rang one locally who was able to give me Doreen's number. I rang her and introduced myself and she agreed to come over and meet me and see the video that I had been shown before I went out.

Half an hour later she turned up. She was a bit older than me, and was a pleasant looking woman with a lovely smile. I let her watch the video alone while I waited downstairs and she came down and said simply that yes, she would come. She then added that it was lucky that I rang today because tomorrow she was due to leave for three weeks in Canada with the W.I.

I realised what a narrow window of chance it was finding Doreen. It seemed extraordinary that Peter, who I had never met, and who just happened to be going to Romania had come over the day before he left and mentioned he knew someone who might come to join me, and then Judy, who I hardly knew and who had never rung me before, should ring up to tell me she could not come at just at the moment needed for me to ask Peter the name of his contact. Leaving me one day to arrange things with Doreen before she left, and by the time she came back I would be gone. With hindsight later I was even more in awe of God's timing as it became clear that Doreen was a very important player in God's plans for Romania.

Ten days later when I returned to Romania. I had a lovely surprise when I found that Nicky Gumble had sent me a signed copy of his book 'A challenging lifestyle'. The snow had gone, and some of the willows along the Danube had begun to sprout.

In the orphanage I found that Alin had not deteriorated, in fact he had gained a bit of weight. As Arlena, the educator, had been left some money and asked to feed him while I was away and she had done so, in fact she shovelled in more food than I had previously dared to. (Obviously I had been a bit over cautious about making him vomit if I overloaded his shrunken stomach)

I started walking home from the orphanage by a roundabout route. After the streets of small wooden shacks I skirted the communist blocs until I came to the remains of the old Braila alongside the Danube. Here the houses were elegant and ornate, but they reminded me of Miss Haversham's wedding cake in the old film of 'Great Expectations' as they were crumbling into ruins, but even so it was a change from the deadly drabness of the rest of the town.

After a few weeks, though I hardly realised it, I was becoming deeply depressed. Things at the orphanage seemed worse. Also Anthea was hardly coming in any more as Ionel had stopped going in to the shipyard and they spent a great deal of their time either in their room, or out visiting his family and friends. I did understand Anthea's reluctance to continue trying to help the children. She had been doing it for far longer than me and had reached the end of her endurance. Sometimes I could hear her desperate sobbing as she told Ionel about her struggles to improve things and gradually realising that the children's conditions were getting worse not better.

I was finding it increasingly hard to go in on my own. Since I came back I had found quite a few children had gone, and when I enquired where they were I was told casually "e moriti" [is dead] and so many of the others had deteriorated, because I now knew them personally I could see the change. Mostly the staff seemed to ignore me, and now did not try to curb their many small acts of callousness.

Their values seemed totally upside down. No one bothered if the children developed oozing sores on their bottoms from being forced to sit on tin potties for hours, but got fussed if a table was moved a foot. I was saddened that all the boxes of toys that had been donated from Britain were stacked up in our room virtually untouched. The few simple toys we took up to the salons had to be locked up when we left, as anything left for the children to play with had disappeared by next morning.

One morning I sat in the kitchen waiting for the time to leave, and I felt totally unable to face another session there on my own. I looked at my watch – another 4 minutes before I must get up and walk out of the door. I thought I might be getting a bit of a sore throat.....*"perhaps it would not be a good idea to go in with a sore throat?...NO...don't kid yourself... I do *not* have a sore throat...I must get up and go...I must make my legs carry me out of this door and on to the orphanage...in...three minutes now"* I looked around and saw that there was a little sticker low down on the fridge Susan had been in the habit of putting little stickers around – I leant forward and read.

'Nothing can happen today that you and I together can't handle.'

Relief flooded me – I was not alone – and I was up and out of the door before I knew it. That relief lasted some time and then depression flooded back.

CHAPTER TEN

This three months session was harder than the first. Then, everything had been so different from home that I had found it fascinating: Now I was feeling very isolated, and I struggled with increasing loneliness. The only way I felt could stop the negative thoughts that had begun to churn around inside my head was to write them down, I was very aware that these unhappy thoughts were not productive and made everything harder, but I seemed unable to stop them.

I have included some of these writings because it makes sense when, after a bit, God very directly helped me to get out of that circle of miserable thoughts.

The first is a letter I wrote to my close friends David and Shiela shortly after I returned to Braila.

"OK Sit back – take a deep breath and prepare yourselves for a good long grumble because you are either going to get a grumble or nothing at all and I've decided that you are going to get the grumble for the simple reason that it helps me......

......I started this letter on Friday but thankfully it no longer applies so much because I packed my bags and took my sleeping bag and went off to Brasov which is in the middle of the mountain district. The lorry driver who delivered some boxes had told me that there was an old couple of missionaries from Devon who let out their large house to Christian groups or individuals. When I got there they were just leaving, I was a bit disappointed to find myself again in a town and asked the way to get to the countryside, and to my great surprise and pleasure they asked me if I would like to accompany them to their other place in a village in the mountains.

It was absolutely beautiful, like stepping back into the pastoral idyll of the middle ages – draught oxen with carts of sweet smelling hay – wide grassy roads with flocks of geese. I expected a younger son, off to win the princess, to appear around the corner as it was so purely picture book.

My hosts had to go out, but I spent the rest of Saturday afternoon and evening just sitting in their orchard drinking in the peace and beauty and on Sunday went with them to their tiny wooden church, again a very memorable experience where a kind elderly doctor from Brasov preached about the gifts of the spirit from 1 Corinthians. Then we were asked to lunch by a village family, and had a nice Romanian meal with these good simple people and it felt very warm and welcoming and I loved being there. Then back to Brasov where the good Doctor showed me the old town, and suggested I come to work in Brasov. "We have children in need too." Then he put me on my train. All very spoiling and nice. It was also I feel answer to prayer – by the end of the second week back you can see by the top section I was having problems.

It's nice when people in England say that we are doing good work but it does not feel like that here. Sometimes when one gets down or runs out of energy one feels so inadequate.

The trouble is that these children have such a simple understanding and when one has had a happy time cuddling, playing or singing with them, then the next time they see you, of course they want the same again and get heartbroken when I pick up a different child. In trying to spread myself to all the children who I feel need comforting I am invariably hurting and rejecting some who feel I am their special Gran.

When there are two of us we can remain upstairs among them all, but when it is just me, as it is now most of the time, I am so overwhelmed by pleading clutching arms that I have to grab the 2 or so most needy and take them to somewhere away from the others leaving tears behind me – it gets very stressful.

I am also battling with the more negative side of my nature as I find I am resenting Ionel and the way he dominates Anthea. She has only worked with the children 2 days since I have been back. His work at the shipyard is very variable and he has only worked 2 days also. They have been very involved with wedding plans, and I do understand it, but the work, though short hours is the most difficult thing I have ever tried to do just because it is so *important* . This is all the children have, this awful reality that they live in 24 hours a day.

When I am not working I spend most of my time alone, I do get cross with my brain that keeps coming up with grumbly thoughts. I know that I am a bit disappointed because Anthea and I work so well as a team when we are both concentrating on the children together. I find myself being resentful about small unimportant things and having to keep mentally slapping my wrist because I realise that it is this disappointment that is making me feel let down and somehow my brain seems to be looking for fuel to feed this feeling. I know that it is so wrong and can only cause disharmony. Thankfully I don't think Anthea and Ionel have a clue that I am having these problems as they are so involved with each other and their approaching wedding and I feel it is important to keep it that way.

Though, by writing these problems, I do feel much happier than I did before I went to Brasov. By the end of last week I felt I was hanging on by my fingernails – and tears were very near the surface all the time. The lovely weekend was an answer to a prayer.

I sometimes feel God does to us what I am trying to do to the children, and when things get grim a bit of comfort is given.

I have to remember that when things are getting difficult I must not make them worse by anticipating them either getting worse or going on forever. I tend to do both these things and so you end up carrying not just the present difficulty but also the imagined future ones. Not a good idea.

Love Caroline "

However I continued to struggle, and again tried to dispel the unhappiness by writing it down.

14th June

"The problem is loneliness – why do lonely people lie on their beds? Reading Adrian Plass's account struck a chord as there he was, horribly lonely, lying on his bed trying to understand about God and the world etc And there was I, also on my bed with such a fellow feeling. EXCEPT – I know that this is temporary, unlike him who has his whole life to sort out, I know that my real life is very unlonely – absolutely bursting in fact with things to do, people to see and talk to and love: So full that I sometimes long for a quiet space.

Now every afternoon and evening I have that quiet space and have to make decisions on how to fill it, that is something that never happens at home – time just fills up there of its own accord.

I mainly read, slowly, stopping to think about what I have read. On the whole I find this very rewarding because all the 22 books I brought out with me this time are ones that have been carefully picked either by myself or friends.

Yesterday Lumitsa and Arlena and I got four children ready for a trip to the park. It is a long time since we last did this, and it was fun. It did not matter that the two girls chatted together in Romanian which I did not understand, because the children were enjoying themselves, and the sunlight, trees and grasses was so marvellous to see. They are unused to uneven surfaces and tumble a lot in the concealed dips in the long grass, and one happy moment came when both Gianna and Nicusha tipped into a hollow and Gianna, getting up first held out her hand to Nicusha – so natural but unseen normally in the orphanage. Then they clustered around for drinks and a sweet each, and tried jumping off the large sculptured stones that decorate this part of the park.

They need a lot of help as climbing onto stones is so novel for them that they are very clumsy and unbalanced – but they enjoyed it. Claudia is very frightened of grass, and screams when you try to put her on to it, so she had to be carried off the path and sat on a stone surrounded by grass, quite like a shipwrecked mariner on one of the tiny islands loved by cartoonists! Then back to the orphanage to feed Alin.

I find the times I notice the loneliness are when I am not absolutely alone – just separate – I buy all the food but increasingly we don't eat together – like yesterday, when I got home from the orphanage, I had a sleep after fixing myself a bite to eat. When I woke I could tell Anthea and Ionel were back in their room so I read on my balcony, later going into the kitchen I found them sitting having a meal. The rest of the evening they were in their room watching television and I was in mine.

I understand how a young engaged couple need to be alone and I'm sure if I was at home I would never even notice the lack of their company. I think it gets a bit out of proportion because I do not know anyone else. Anthea is really the only person who can understand the daily assaults on one's heart caused by the things one sees at the orphanage but can do nothing about – endless small cruelties and large sufferings. Someone might say, how could I, seeing such appalling deprivation bother about my own loneliness, and I am very much aware how wonderful and free and blessed my normal life is."

This last entry was written during a *very low* time, shortly before I had an experience walking home that helped me continue:

'I am still surprised by my increasing hunger to read about Christ. Somehow there is an edge of desperation in this reading. I am aware that I need help in order to cope – help to overcome the loneliness, anger and negative thoughts that grumble and rumble inside me.

I compare the lives of the early Christians, Paul and his companions with my comfortable life here and there is no comparison – I know it, and it does help, but the thoughts and feelings that give me most problems are not directly about myself but are caused by things in Romania that I can't change and can't accept gracefully."

Shortly after writing these accounts of my struggles, God intervened in a very direct way. It happened when I was walking home from the orphanage along the Danube and I passed a bench under a Willow tree and sat down. The leaves of the willow were now fully out and swayed in the breeze. I sat there quietly looking at the cracks in the pavement when I heard a voice in my head. It said,

"You know what you are doing, don't you. You are looking at all the things that are wrong and cruel and collecting them up to feed your misery." I sat very still. The voice was not a big GOD voice, it was gentle and loving and almost amused – and it was *not* me – then it went on…

"….and you are beginning to look at the children's suffering from the point of view of how much it hurts *you* to see them suffer."

I suddenly realised that it was true – that was *just* what I was doing – it was like a ray of light breaking into my dark mind, like a splash of joy. The voice seemed to say, but no longer in words "…at last she's seen it…."

Everything around me, the tree, the river, the cracks in the pavement seemed so clear that I can remember them exactly, even now years later.

Then I got up, with my heart filled with joy. I walked home saying "Thank you...thank you...thank you...thank you" again and again, and then finally a heartfelt prayer. "Please never let me be overwhelmed by self pity like that again."

It was a turning point, and I never found myself swept away by that sort of misery again. I had never really understood the bit in the Bible about strapping on God's armour but now I realised that was what had happened – though in this case it was strapped on for me.

CHAPTER ELEVEN

I had begun to realise that Ionel and Anthea were beginning to make other plans about their future. I felt a bit hurt not to be told what they were thinking of doing, but I knew that Ionel had the Romanian tendency to keep things secret – understandable after years of communist rule.

I continued going into the orphanage, though now mostly on my own. It was apparent that things there were getting worse not better. Every morning I would choose which children seemed most in need, and then the first three hours were spent with them. Some just needed rocking and singing, others liked being held while they shook a ring of bells: the skill was to try to tune into what was needed most.

I remembered back to when I first came and realised that I no longer noticed the smells, and though I deplored the way the children had to lie so often in their wet soiled clothes I was not personally put off handling them. And it seemed like a small miracle as I realised these negative reactions had vanished without any effort on my part. It made the work so much easier. And it felt like a gift from God.

There was one boy, Gheorgu, who had at first seemed repellently ugly with rotten teeth and fetid breath. He was one of those who clung desperately whenever we appeared. I found that Gheorgu loved to sit on my lap facing me, our arms around each other's backs, while we rocked to and fro in time to me singing 'see saw Marjorie Daw…etc' over and over again. In one of these rocking sessions his eyes looked into mine with a look so open and guileless that my heart melted and I felt pure love flow between us, just as it had when one of my own babies had first looked into my eyes.

A few of the children seemed fundamentally bright even though they could not talk, so I would take them down, one at a time to our little room and there one of our favourite things would be to sit on the floor and open up one of the shoe boxes that had been sent out from home. I thought about the child at home who must have chosen these little treasures, and we would slowly take them out, one by one: a gonk with neon pink hair, a bead bracelet that would be put on a small wrist, hair clips that sadly could not be worn if the children had shorn heads, so they would fumblingly try to put them in my hair, and so on.

Then the last hour was spent with Alin. He was still very withdrawn and showed no obvious affection, and he never smiled, but he knew when it was his time and climbed onto me and would sometimes sigh and close his eyes as he leant against me and that was enough. Now he was no longer tied in his cot I found that when I put him to bed at the end of the morning, and put a wafer biscuit in his hand and covered his head with a bit of cloth he would snuggle down almost happily in his own private world. Each child was different and I had grown to love them.

I remembered how it had been in the spring when Anthea was still coming in regularly, and how, for the first time on a Friday we had dressed a few children up in clothes that Anthea had put by and ordered a taxi to take us to the park. The children had never been outside before, and after we had put down a rug we encouraged them to walk on the grass. Some managed it with their arms held out for balance, moving like an elderly person crossing a heaving deck, and when they reached the nearest tree they clung to it before attempting the walk back to the rug. I remembered Claudia who was genuinely frightened of the grass and screamed if set down on it. And the picnic which took some planning as the children had only ever eaten the liquid potato and vegetable mush, so the first time I offered each one a chocolate Smartie they all spat it out before they could taste it, and I realised these smarties must have seemed strange and hard, nothing like food as they knew it.

I remembered how every day we had tried to get some protein into their diet, crumbling up the Romanian feta like cheese, or bringing in some finely minced chicken to incorporate in their food, and Anthea had been given a case of baby food and we used it to feed the ones who were very weak. Remembering these times I wondered what would happen now.

One of the things I held on to was my initial instructions to "feed my lambs" which I felt was to just feed and care for the children, they were my lambs – just that and nothing more – I was *sure* I was not to get involved politically.

One day, when I was alone in the flat, it was very hot and I went to sit in a cold bath (we always kept some water in the bath to flush the loo,) and I came back into my room, and was mildly surprised to see my bible lying open face down in the middle of the floor. I picked it up, wondering vaguely how it had got to be there, and idly glanced at the open page. There were four psalms, (I had not read the psalms yet,) and my eye fell on a verse in psalm 82 – and I read verses 2-5

How long will you defend the unjust
And show partiality to the wicked?
Defend the cause of the weak and fatherless;
Maintain the rights of the poor and oppressed.
Rescue the weak and needy;
Deliver them from the hand of the wicked.
They know nothing, they understand nothing.
They walk about in darkness;
All the foundations of the earth are shaken.

Again it was like an electric charge and I found myself covered in goose pimples as I read the words – they were speaking directly to me – I knew I would have to obey them and not just care for the children. I was being told to fight for them.

But I did not know how I was to do it.

CHAPTER TWELVE

A few weeks later things came to a head in the orphanage. Anthea and Ionel decided to go and confront Dr Stefan personally, with Ionel translating as Anthea spoke no Romanian and Dr. Stefan spoke very little English. I was at home with a heavy cold which turned out to be a good thing, because things went very wrong. It started out with Ionel translating Anthea's words, but quickly developed into a row between the two men with Anthea standing by looking on helplessly, and the upshot of this was that they were forbidden to come in any more. Because I had not been present I was not included in this ban. (I realised that there are some advantages to being older, you are not considered a threat and are often overlooked.) I realised that Dr Stefan had not listened to any of Anthea's concerns, as he was so angry with Ionel. What bothered him, he told me indignantly, was the right of a low paid shipyard worker to criticise someone in authority like himself. Also he was convinced that Ionel was only with Anthea in order to get to England – and had said so.

Now, with Anthea and Ionel making plans that would not involve me, I wondered what my next move should be. Clearly we were outstaying our welcome at Braila but I had committed myself to spending a year in Romania.

I remembered that I had seen a leaflet among Anthea's things about eleven rescued children who now lived in two houses in a village called Harja in Transylvania. They were looked after by an English girl called Charlotte Budd who had worked in

Chernavoda with Anthea. The photos of happy children romping on a grassy hillside had looked lovely, but when I had asked Anthea about it she had said that you could not get there from here.

Now I remembered that leaflet, and I'm ashamed to say because Anthea and Ionel were being so secretive about their future plans I felt resentful, and when they were out I thought I would go into their room and find the leaflet.

But all I can say is that I was not allowed to. It's difficult to describe how this was so – but it was very clear – so, when Anthea and Ionel were leaving for their wedding in England I remembered the leaflet and asked Anthea whether I might see it as I was wondering if they might need a helper there. She immediately got it and once again we felt close, and I was again aware what a lovely person she was, and was so grateful that I had not gone behind her back.

Then they left and I was alone. I had planned to write immediately to Mary Gibson who had raised the money to build these two houses in Harja and was financing them. But thankfully it did not happen because I still nurtured some resentment towards Ionel who had become very controlling, and because this resentment seemed to set the tone of my thoughts I am sure it would have shown in the letter. But I was prevented from writing it because I had a visitor.

Some weeks before I had been standing in the bread queue and I noticed a young man who looked very different from the Romanians who all wore sombre clothes and had short dark hair. This fellow had a long blond pony-tail and was slightly hippy looking. He was called Jud and was an American Peace Corps worker teaching English at the High School. It was quite exciting as this was the first time either of us had met another person from the West and we became immediate friends. That first evening he walked me home along the Danube, talking all the way, and then because we were still talking we walked back along the river again and then home once more, where I invited him in for coffee. Anthea was friendly but Ionel took an instant dislike to him and said he could not come again. I found this irritating as I now paid the rent and all the household expenses. But Ionel expected to be obeyed, and to keep the peace, and because I did not want to upset Anthea I did not argue.

Now, as soon as they left, Jud turned up, so off we went for a long walk in the nearby park and had a snack lunch out, then more walking and talking until it was evening, ending up back at my flat. He continued to stay on chatting so I got us a bit of supper. I expected him to go then so I could write my letter to Mary Gibson, but rather surprisingly, considering our age difference, he stayed until late discussing our favourite music and I played him some of my tapes. When at last he left, instead of tackling the letter I went to bed. Early next morning I awoke with the complete letter in my head and any trace of negative feelings had vanished – blown away it seemed by my happy companionable day.

The next week was very happy, Jud and his Romanian girlfriend, Anna, took me under their wings and introduced me to their other young Romanian friends and I was included in all their doings. It was great fun. One evening we all ran along the edge of the river throwing a Frisbee to each other as we ran, some even jumped into the mud to retrieve it. Then they looked at their black legs and realised that because the water would be cut off they would not be able to rinse it off. That was where my bath of water became useful and they all crowded into my flat and took it in turns to rinse off the mud. It was wonderful to hear laughter and high spirits for the first time in that flat.

After that week was up I took the train to Bucharest to meet Doreen. She arrived with her cine camera. and over the course of the next month she recorded the condition of the children. The good thing was that both of us, being old, were not considered important. Just two harmless batty old foreigners and so no one went to any trouble to hide the true state of affairs in the way they usually did if outsiders came.

Doreen was shocked but resolute and it was great to once more share the work with another person.

One day, when we were going downstairs, we saw that one of the stray dogs was lying on the landing. As we approached it looked desperately right and left and dragged itself further back against the wall and we guessed that it had a broken leg. It was quite a young dog with shaggy yellow fur, and was very thin, and we realised that it must have crawled through the broken pane at the entrance door. The next day it was still there and Doreen remembered that we had some food left over from our supper and went back to get it. As the dog seemed so frightened, and we did not want to cause it any more pain, we left the food on the stairs and went on to work. When we returned the dog was still there but the food was gone. There were no vets in Braila and we did not know how to help it, but we continued leaving food and water and gradually it seemed less frightened, it just watched us warily, but did not move. We never tried touching it, and noticed that it left no mess and realised that at night it must drag itself out.

I had heard from Mary Gibson who wrote to suggest I visit Harja and meet Charlotte. And so one weekend, half way through that month, we took a very early train and made the long journey North to Onesti where Charlotte met us in the Land Rover and drove us the 27 kilometers to Harja.

The village of Harja was set in a wide river valley, and on either side tracks led up the slopes where some parts were wooded and other parts were meadow. We were met by the children who were very excited to see us. They were beautifully dressed and attended by smiling Romanian helpers.

That Saturday it was very hot and we took the children to the stream where they stripped to their pants and splashed in the water, while over a small bonfire meat patties were being cooked for a picnic.

Later I walked by myself up the hillside and struggled with a confusing jumble of thoughts. I was so attracted to this place, but was it because it was so beautiful and unspoiled and the children were happy?

I so wanted to get it right, but I did not trust myself and I had no sense about what God wanted me to do – perhaps He had other plans for me – this place seemed like heaven after Braila, so did I want to come here because of that? Finally I said a small prayer asking God to make it very clear if I should come here.

That evening Charlotte suggested taking Doreen and me for a walk up the hillside. At first she meant just the three of us, but all the children wanted to come, so quite a troupe of us started to climb the zig zag road. Some of the children cut the corners and scrambled up the steep, more direct slope to the road above, but one little girl, Andra, was not able to keep up. She was tiny and underweight so I picked her up and settled her on my hip and looked up to the road above and wondered whether to climb up the direct path or follow the road around.

Above me Charlotte was looking down. The setting sun made a halo of light through her hair and her face was in shadow. Suddenly I remembered that this had happened before. I had stood like this, holding a small child, and looked up at someone above exactly as I was doing now. Then I remembered my dreams – It was just the same as one of my dreams – that's why I recognised it so clearly. Charlotte later told me that when she stood there looking down she felt that God was telling her that I would come to help her in the autumn.

Back in Braila Doreen and I continued going into the orphanage, and one day on our way home we went to look at an enormous church that was being built with money provided by American Baptists – it was a great deal of money. We were shown around the half finished site by the Pastor while he outlined his ambitious plans. He was so excited about this new church.

When we got back Doreen was very quiet and then announced that she was going back to see him. She took some photographs of the children and showed them to him. She said he winced as he looked at them, and said that when his church was built, only then could he think about the children.

Before our last day Doreen took her cine camera into the orphanage, and because no one paid any attention to us now, she was able to film the reality of the children's lives, and just before we left for home she popped into the lower salon where the older children were confined in their cots. The film was very poignant as the children's faces lit up at the sight of Doreen and those whose hands were free held them out to her. She quickly filmed how every child was tied to the bars and how most of the cots did not even have mattresses, just oil cloth over the cot's wire bases. This film, unknown to us then, was to become an essential asset in the later fight to get things changed.

It was late August now and the end of my second three months stay was nearly over. Soon it would be time for Doreen and me to leave. I knew that that was the end; I would not be coming back. We were no longer welcome.

It was a time of heart searching – had we done any good at all? We had grown to love the children but now we were leaving them. Would it have been better if they had never felt our love – just to have it taken away? Would they look out for us? We had left them before but had always come back. Now that would not happen. So the expectation of going home and seeing our families was tinged with a confusing sadness. We even had regrets about the yellow dog when we gave him a special last feed. Like with the children we could not explain why we were leaving.

Once again I was helped as I struggled with these doubts, as one day I suddenly had a deep conviction about God's forgiving love. It was so strong that I wrote it down so as not to forget it.

'I believe God *really* loves people who feel they are unworthy, grieves for our anguish and guilt and longs to help us.

I think that God realises that *our* awareness of our unworthiness is the greatest block to approaching him.

That's why he said *repeatedly* "I took your sin" and he longs to break through this barrier of guilt and self doubt. He wants to carry it for us so we can feel free to understand his love. We have to try to trust that he will do what he says.'

Years later with hindsight, I was to realise why it was important for us to be there, even if not for our children there, but eventually for others who we would never know. Sadly we were not able to change the lives of the children we grew to love in Braila. But their suffering, when exposed to the world caused such shock that it started a chain of events that years later would bring about profound changes for the better – not just in Braila – but, I was told later, in the forty odd similar establishments for 'irrecupables' throughout Romania.

Our Bloc

Anthea walking to the Orphanage

Approaching the Orphanage

The Orphanage

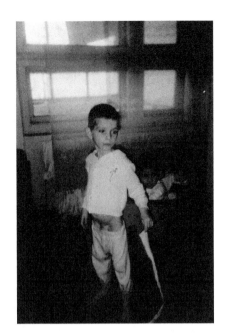

Alin - November 1996

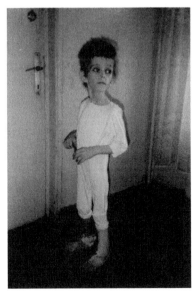

Alin - 4 months later

Me with Vasile aged 5 and Alin aged 10

Marius

Monel with no mattress or bedding

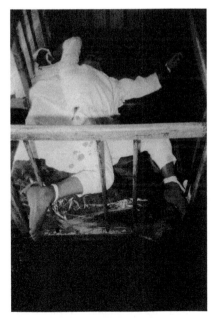

Romeka who was nearly always tied as she was very active

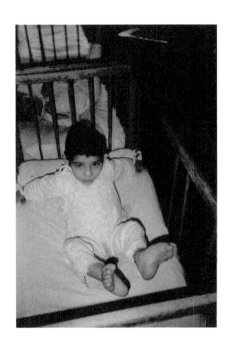

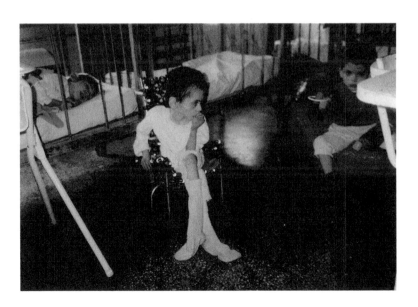

On potties

In the park

HARJA

Chapter Thirteen

During my month at home I met Mary Gibson and it was agreed that I should go out to help Charlotte.

So in October I was again off to Romania, but this time to Transylvania. At Bucharest I caught the train that travels all the way up the Eastern side of Romania and Charlotte met me at Onesti with the Land Rover, and as we drove to Harja the first snowfall of the winter fluttered around us. The wooded hills, with their dusting of frost, the small villages and wooden houses that we passed through would become very familiar but then I was awestruck by the beauty.

The two houses at Harja were identical. Basically one storey, but with a platform overlooking the main living area which we used as the office, and off this platform were two little rooms under the eaves. These were used for general storage, but one was also my bedroom, while Charlotte slept in a similar attic in the other house. The children slept in the two bedrooms downstairs.

The first week was getting to know the staff, and most importantly, the children in my house. There were four boys and two girls. The two oldest boys were 5 and were called Marius and Luci. Marius was unusual in being fair haired, he was reserved and quite formal and sort of reminded me of a German u-boat commander from old war movies. His friend Luci was amazingly beautiful. Luci was quite shy and was also reserved but I noticed that he was very kind to the younger ones.

Flori was a year older, she was the house's little mother, I was told she was not very good at school work, but I noticed she was practical She loved clearing the table and helping the staff, and she was encouraging to the other children..

Then came two younger boys, Silviu and Vasili. Four year old Silviu was fair and had long eyelashes that were often covered with sleepy dust, he seemed happy to play on his own and seemed to be on that cusp between babyhood and childhood. Vasili was said to be from gypsy stock. He was dark with curly hair, and when he was little he had been found sitting half naked in a cardboard box in the snow, so no one knew his exact age.

He was easily frightened and needed a lot of reassurance, and occasionally some unconscious memory of hunger made him stuff his mouth so full of bread that he could not close his lips, but neither could he chew or swallow, so his anxious eyes stared out above his bulging cheeks as he was so reluctant to let any of it go.

The smallest of all the children was Andra who was four, she was a tiny little girl, and like all the children she never whined or cried, unless something physically hurt her, but unlike the others; who ate everything, Andra did not want to either talk or eat. When Doreen and I were there for that weekend in the summer Andra would only eat tomatoes, but now she had added salami to her menu. She indicated that she wanted some by bending her arm at the elbow and flexing it back and forth like a caricature of a strong man, and the staff always gave her some. They were wonderful with her, never fussing her when she would not eat, but encouraging her with smiles and cries of delight if she did eat something. I remembered how, when Doreen and I had visited, she was the child that I had picked up and tucked over my hip as we climbed the hill that first evening, when I had suddenly realised that it had all happened before in one of my dreams.

The children were very well behaved, I never heard anyone answer back or be rude, sometimes at meal times some of them, like Vasile, would stuff so much bread into their mouths that they could not swallow it, but I noticed that this anxiety about food was beginning to disappear and, with the exception of Andra, they ate everything and there was no waste.

Curiously I had heard that children who were rescued from the sort of horrors that these children had experienced, and been adopted, were often very difficult to care for as they were emotionally unstable and were subject to rages and destructive tantrums. But I never saw anything like that with our children; perhaps because they were like a family. They supported each other at school if anyone was bullied, and they were noticeably happy, often singing at the tops of their voices in the car, and during their games outside. But they were not spoilt. The timetable of their lives was very ordered, bedtimes and a rest time after lunch were not negotiable, and they were obedient because like all Romanians, it seemed, they accepted authority without question.

Charlotte's house had a family of two sisters and a brother. Florina the oldest of all the children was eight (going on eighteen). She was self assured and flirty, and always hungry for attention and admiration. Her sister Ancuta was two years younger and was very different, she was quietly intelligent and unselfish, and I admired her and always felt that if we had been a similar age we would have been friends. Then there was their younger brother, Elvis, (pronounced Yellvis) who was five. He was a volatile firecracker of a boy, and the only child with an undercurrent of violence. But he was also very good looking and could be charming. He, like Florina, played up to any visitors, and needed to be the centre of attention. These children had been abandoned by their parents and been placed in an orphanage, and, like all the other children, had suffered, but unlike all the others, who seemed happy and settled, I felt Florina and Elvis were unstable emotionally.

Then there was five year old Corina, a pretty little girl who had been put in an orphanage when her parents had gone off to work in Hungary. And finally Alina also five, who was profoundly deaf from untreated ear infections during her babyhood in an orphanage. Both she and Andra would have failed their assessments at three years old and would have been sent to somewhere like Braila if they had not been rescued.

I did not keep a diary; life was too busy, but occasionally I jotted down my first impressions to be used in letters home. Like the following:

"I have been here nearly a month now, and am feeling much more settled and at home. Also I am starting to see in which ways I am able to help. I was warned that the staff do not take kindly to people who arrive and usurp their roles – so I kept a low profile to start with, and have been very impressed by their commitment and dedication. They work on a rota basis and really do all the everyday caring of the children, so I was right in imagining my input with the children would be more in the grandmother role, especially as only Charlotte and I live here full time with the children.

I now do quite a lot of the driving. Last week the village school in Harja was shut down and teacher and pupils were moved to the next village and no transport was provided – The day starts with scraping the frost off the windscreen of our large ex naval Land Rover at 7.45 and then it is packed with eleven of our children, and seven from the village. The children are left in a little log cabin schoolroom with its tile stove and little desks and slates and toys; it's just playschool at their age and they seem to love it. It takes two of these trips to get them all there, and at twelve I get them all back.

In the morning as I drive back I see the life of the village starting and find this fascinating – passing a Jack and Jill type well there are two women talking, their hands tucked in their sleeves for warmth, their dark shapeless clothes look as if they could come from any era. Then I pass a old man with a stick driving his five geese to graze the school's grassy playground.

Near home I see a woman coming out of her front gate with her few sheep to take to the shepherd. He is a strange looking figure covered from head to toe in a vast cloak made of long hairy fleece like a tent, and his head covered in a high black hat.

I have had to drive to Onesti and back twice in the last 2 days, it's 27 km away, and I find the responsibility of these trips makes me quite nervous and I say a quick prayer before we set off. It feels much more dangerous than driving at home because of all the four legged traffic, mainly horses and carts, or oxen pulling carts so heaped up with maize stalks that they are like wide haystacks creeping down the road. There are old men in donkey carts trotting down the middle of the road, and lots of impatient thundering lorries, and a few wild drivers in clapped out Dacias and the odd drunken cyclist all on bendy icy mountainous roads. Today we passed a walking funeral procession with a poor old lady carried in an open coffin on a bier. Then this afternoon we all walked to the church with candles to have one of the children baptised, and finally, this evening, driving the new godparents back to Onesti, we passed a walking wedding party with the bride leading the way – all of life walking down the road in one day!

Unlike Braila, where English was our main language, I am totally surrounded by the Romanian way of life and am the only person who does not speak Romanian. Charlotte is completely fluent, and no one in my house speaks English.

The children seem so happy here, they don't seem the least concerned that I hardly understand anything that they say, but seem to like to cuddle up and are very affectionate. My main role is helping Charlotte, I have such admiration for her ability to cope with the mind boggling bureaucracy and all the things that need to be done when there are 11 children and two homes and staff. Eye tests for two – a chest x ray for one who had TB once (thankfully he is now clear) and all the hundreds of things to remember in order to keep everything happy and running well, so I am beginning to take over the responsibility for a few of these. Charlotte says she would not be able to continue without someone to share it with, so, though the work is totally different from Braila I still feel it is necessary.

We had the first snowstorm 2 weeks ago, and Charlotte driving someone to the station in the early morning went out of control on black ice and rolled over and over down the steep bank ending upside down in the river below. They found themselves hanging upside down in their seatbelts with their heads touching the water. They managed to drop down and kick out the windscreen and scramble out. They were shaken and had some small cuts but otherwise were all right. Later, when we looked at the jeep lying upside down in the river we realised how different it might have been – how two very remarkable things had saved their lives. We saw that where they had come off the road was the one place where the saplings were small and bendy enough to slow them down as they rolled down the bank, and the jeep had landed on a shallow spit reaching out into the river, while a few feet on either side the water was deeper and swiftly flowing. The Arow was a write off but luckily Enterprise oil, who help a lot, gave us one they had no need of, so we were back to two cars again.

News of the situation at the orphanage in Braila is still not good though my photographs have now been seen by some influential people who are shocked and promising to help. When I look at these happy children and consider what their fates might have been, it seems so strange they just happened to be in the orphanage that Mary Gibson visited, out of hundreds of similar orphanages, and were the right age."

CHAPTER FOURTEEN

Life settled down into a pattern, I in my house with my six children and Charlotte next door with her five, and a rota of helpers coming in daily. I was struck by the difference between these helpers here, and the ones I had known at Braila. In both cases they were just local women who had needed a job – no qualifications were asked for – but here, where the whole atmosphere created by Charlotte was based around nurturing love, they responded with real loving warmth towards the children. Each house had a rota system with two members of staff always on duty. They were responsible for all the day to day care of the children, and each day followed a very rigid pattern. I noticed that Romanian people seemed to need definite rules set out, and then they followed them unquestioningly without any deviation or flexibility.

Every night, on a rota basis, two helpers slept together on the sofa bed in the living room so they were there in the morning to rekindle the fire, dress the children and get the breakfast which was always bread and margarine. Two old 'aunties' who each kept a cow took it in turns to deliver milk in old coca cola bottles, (these bottles were very prized and were never thrown away and were used for years). Then the children were taken to school or kindergarten in the next village in the Land Rover. When it was cold I had to remember to go out early to plug a long lead from the generator into a socket under the Land Rover's bonnet so that by school time the engine would be warm enough to start. Sometimes an old lady, with her little rosy face almost covered by a headscarf, would climb in beside me and make the sign of a cross as we started off. I also said a prayer as I felt that driving a car packed with children over icy roads was an enormous responsibility.

Directly breakfast was over an enormous pan of water was placed on the stove, with just a handful of finely chopped peppers that had been salted down in the autumn, which gave it a characteristic sour taste. Then sometimes a small scraggy chicken was added and boiled up for a while and then chopped up and put in the oven. Then it was all left to cool so that by the time I had collected the children at twelve it was just tepid. Both houses always ate separately but with much the same menu, first the soup and bread followed by a pile of yellow maize meal, called mamaliga, with either a bit of sausage or the chicken on top. This way, one small chicken could adequately feed nine of us, the two Romanian helpers, me and the six children. The children seldom had anything sweet unless visitors brought them sweets or we occasionally bought little wafer biscuits in town. Though there were no fresh vegetables, and very little variety we all kept extremely well all winter.

I went with Charlotte to visit an old woman in the village who was willing to sell us apples from her orchard, and would let us store them in her cellar. As we walked among the trees she pointed to some broken branches and grumbled about how the bears came down at night and broke the branches to get at the apples. These apples were to last us all winter, though by spring it was a problem to find an unblemished one as rats had bitten into most of them and spat chewed apple mush over everything. We just washed them and cut out the chewed bits.

I loved the simplicity of the life here. Everyone in the village kept a few animals in their yards. Every morning the shepherd would collect the sheep in ones and twos from the individual houses and take them up into the hills to graze. Then in the evening he would bring them back and each sheep would peel off when it came to its own yard, just like children home from school. There they stayed all night along with a few poultry and a pig. Some of these pigs were housed above the ground on a surface of spaced out branches, so that all their dung and urine fell through the gaps and ran away. It was sensible and avoided them having to lie in their own muck, but looked quite uncomfortable as the branches were uneven and knobbly.

Later that winter, when we walked through the snowy village we would come across large patches of snow that had curdled up into a frothy redness, and the signs that a straw fire had singed the dead pig's hairs, as each household prepared their year's supply of meat.

Every family had a strip of land where they grew the maize for mamaliga and animal fodder and brought it home piled high on their carts, pulled by oxen or horses that were lean and sinewy, very different from the heavy farm horses of Britain. Some of them had a red tuft of wool on their harness to ward off evil spirits.

Every day I admired Charlotte more. She was resourceful and never grumbled. But the most noticeable thing about her was the way she radiated love and fun. Throughout the winter we would often take the children up into the hills for picnics – always lighting a little fire, and sometimes only getting back after dark. I imagine the staff found this strange to start with, but they entered into the spirit of it and seemed to enjoy it as much as the children. We never saw anyone else up there except sometimes we would see the shepherd trudging slowly by, a lonely slightly sinister figure; followed by the villager's sheep and a scruffy depressed looking dog. He always ignored us, and often a sort of silence fell until he had passed.

When I arrived in October the villagers were organising their next winter's wood. The wood for this winter was already neatly stacked up ready for use. They would take the horse up into the hills and choose a few trees to cut down and drag back, in this way the villagers had kept warm for centuries as it was completely sustainable.

Some of the people still lived in the old way. Their wooden houses were set inside a high fence, surrounding a courtyard of trodden earth with neat stacks of firewood and corncobs. Instead of one larger house there were little separate houses; not much bigger than sheds, that faced onto the courtyard. The summer houses were more open, but the winter house would be very small – often just one room, with hard bench beds covered with colourful rugs and dominated by a huge stove with the inevitable large cooking pot on it, and a table covered in oilcloth. It was crowded and cosy and we were always made welcome. We would sit on the bed and be plied with little hard sweet cakes or sunflower seeds and sometimes tiny glasses of sweet wine. Charlotte, with her fluent Romanian chatted easily while I relied on smiles and nods. These people had no modern conveniences at all. No running water, no taps or sinks or lavatories, no electricity, shops or cars. In fact their lives seemed to have changed very little for hundreds of years, yet it struck me how much these people smiled. I realised that one of the problems about Braila had been that no one ever smiled.

Chapter Fifteen

Things were not always rosy. Like everyone else, wood was our only source of heating. Both our houses had a large modern wood burning stove that was able to heat the whole house, but unlike everyone else we had to buy our wood. A problem arose when Charlotte ordered a load of firewood and then refused it when it was delivered because it was not what they had agreed. She then found it difficult to get wood anywhere else as the man who had tried to cheat her threatened to make life very difficult for anyone who supplied her. Eventually something was sorted out and a huge pile of logs was delivered.

Our houses were very westernised. We had running water pumped up automatically from our own well, and washing machines and dryers and cooking stoves run with electricity from our generator. The only difficulty was if anything broke down there was no one who could fix it, and Charlotte and I spent hours poring over the pump's information leaflets trying to sort out a problem.

I grew very close to some of the staff and was occasionally invited back to their homes. These were very simple and tidy, and were very basic compared to western houses, just an enamel bowl for washing with water drawn from the communal well, and tall tiled wood- burning stoves for all the heating and cooking. The helpers must have enjoyed using the modern equipment and followed their original instructions to the letter. When the children had first come as babies from the orphanage the staff were told to wash everything they wore daily and dry it in the clothes dryer. Years passed but they still automatically washed every bit of clothing every day, even woolly jumpers. The air there was very dry but I only managed to persuade them tactfully to hang clothes on the outside line by showing them that my clothes dried quicker outside than those in the dryer.

Though we had no phone or internet link I was still in touch with my brother Guy by fax, as once a week we drove into Onesti where we were able to receive and send any faxes. Then on to get basic supplies from a warehouse, then to the bakers for baskets of bread, and then – our least favourite job – to the slaughterhouse to buy meat. Once, when I was standing beside the car waiting for Charlotte I began to consider what I was wearing. It was very cold yet I was warm, and as I stood there I started to work out where each garment came from, and I made a note in my diary.

"19th December. Temperature: minus19 degrees centigrade. My thick red socks, given to me by Ben and Elke – vest no.1 was sent to me by Elizebeth O'Dell (a lady from our church,) – vest no.2 was from Pernie (a very beloved aunt). – Shirt from Fanny (my daughter). – Jersey from Sam. – Hood and scarf from Maddy (my best friend). – Gloves from Pernie. – coat from my friend Gillian and hankie from Maddy." And I realised that apart from warming my body all these gifts from loved ones also warmed my heart.

One day Charlotte had to go to Iasi, close to the Russian border, as the customs wanted to see us about our Land Rover. She collected all the appropriate papers – there were so many- all the car's documents, the photocopies of the passport of the driver who had brought it in from England originally, and his documents, the charity's authorisation, and anything else she could think of, and we set off before dawn for the long drive over icy roads. We were all bundled up as the Land Rover had no heating. Then as we crossed high ground it began to snow so we had to stop every few kilometres to clear the windscreen as the wipers did not work. In all it was a long hard drive, but the Land Rover, in spite of its idiosyncrasies was very precious to us.

Iasi was a grey border town, and when we found the custom office it was square, drab and forbidding. We went into a room where six female clerks sat at desks overflowing with piles of brown folders. One nodded to us to wait and then we sat and watched her eat her lunch – a rather dried up looking hunk of bread – finally she got down a folder and asked to see Charlotte's papers. She flicked through them as if she was looking for something, then she found it and we realised that she was looking for any discrepancies. The photocopy of the original driver's passport was smudged and the date was unclear. She then found, after a diligent search, another discrepancy. We watched her anxiously as we knew that if the papers were not in order the customs could fine us a thousand pounds or confiscate the Land Rover and there was nothing we could do about it. Then she started questioning Charlotte in an angry voice, and shouted Charlotte down as she tried to explain. Then after another long period of waiting she said that she would take us to see the boss. Glumly we followed her as she strode ahead to a door at the end of the corridor.

The boss's office, like hers was dingy and utilitarian; just plain grubby concrete walls and floor, and as we walked in we realised that it was not just us but she also was frightened of him. He was sitting at his desk and looked up when we came in and my heart sank. Everything about him was square. He had an almost shaved head and a thin grim line for his lips, and he looked deeply unfriendly. Then they all three started talking loudly as the Romanians stabbed at the papers with accusing fingers. I did not speak enough Romanian to know what it was all about, but I could catch the note of desperate pleading in Charlotte's voice. None of them noticed me, so on the spur of the moment I turned towards the corner and prayed very simply, saying, "Please God save this situation." I turned around and saw that Charlotte had stepped back while the two Romanians went on turning over the papers.

Suddenly I had a thought and whispered to Charlotte if she had any photographs of the children. She thought and then began to look through her briefcase again and right at the bottom was a picture of all the children taken a few years ago, sitting in a row on a long bench – their little legs dangling, just like birds on a telegraph wire. Charlotte took it out and without a word placed it on the desk in front of him. A silence fell, it was as if the loud accusing voices had been cut off with a knife. And the silence went on as he looked and looked. Finally he looked up and said to the woman.

"Why are you making trouble for these people? Sort it out." She gulped in amazement and turned to leave with us following her. I remember how her shoes banged on the floor as she strode down the corridor. Then she opened the office door and said to the others.

"He's mad – he's gone completely mad." They all stopped working and crowded around, then one of them said wonderingly as she looked at our photograph,

"Perhaps he likes children."

But we knew that when he saw the children God must have touched his heart.

One day Charlotte took me to meet two elderly English ladies who lived in a small remote village in another valley. I was interested to meet them as we did not know of any other Western people living locally. They seemed thrilled to see us and I had the impression that they were the last two sisters of a religious order that had died out. They had very little money and so lived very simply, but they radiated a sort of gentle goodness as they showed us the little schoolroom they had set up years earlier for the local children. This small school was their life and they were determined to keep it going as long as the children needed them. It was a happy visit and

I was touched by their dedication and love, both for God and their little pupils.

On another occasion Charlotte told me about a little girl called Susie who had been with them at Harja for some time, and for a reason I was never told, she had to be found somewhere else to live, and finally was sent to a convent run by elderly Romanian nuns. In the daytime it was a school for older children, and little Susie was the only child who lived with the nuns.

Charlotte often visited Susie and suggested I might like to come. We took a bag of little sweets and set off. The first impression was rather bleak; a square concrete building both inside and out, with long dark corridors and closed doors. Susie was very small and bright. She was excited to see us and be given the sweets, but before tasting any she immediately ran off and knocked on one of the doors, inside was a very old fashioned looking schoolroom and a lesson was going on. Susie trotted in and went down the rows of desks putting a sweet on each one, and then up to the nun taking the class and gave her one, then out she came and did the same thing in the next class – every nun she met was given a sweet, and as she did this she skipped with excitement. I saw that it was a joy to her to have something to give. Soon nearly all the sweets were gone and we had to persuade her to have one herself. I realised that my first impression of a dark grim place with elderly nuns dressed in black was just a surface impression, because it was clear that they loved Susie and she loved them. But even so the goodbyes were hard as Susie cried as she hugged Charlotte, and we drove silently home choked up with emotion.

CHAPTER SIXTEEN

One day I had an unexpected windfall. For some years I had run my brother Guy's house in Hartland as a holiday let while he was living in Italy, now he had just sold it for sixty thousand pounds and decided to give me 10%. That meant I had six thousand pounds that I had not expected. I knew I wanted to use it here in Romania but felt concerned about finding the right outlets as I had become aware that a lot of money that had been donated with good heart from England was not followed up, and was misappropriated.

I knew I could not help the children in Braila with money. While Dr.Stefan and the staff had any control of donations we had seen that nothing got through to the children. I decided to ask God to make it very clear how I was – or was not – to use this money. Mentally I handed it over to him.

Meanwhile Charlotte and I were looking for one more child to live in Charlotte's house. So the search was on and we went to the local orphanage in Onesti where babies lived until they were three, then they had a brief assessment before going to the big orphanage, or if they failed; for whatever reason, they went to a place like Braila for the irrecupables.

Here we saw rows of little children sitting on potties and the staff picked out one little boy who was almost three and brought him to us. We all went in another room and they told us that he was called Gabriel. He was very delicate, and was beautiful. His neck seemed as slender as a flower stalk, and he had large intelligent solemn eyes. The staff encouraged him to show us how clever he was, and made him recite a small poem. I was aware how much more caring the staff were compared to Braila. They seemed really fond of their charges even though lack of money and facilities made it a grim place.

They told us that when Gabriel was a baby he and his older brother were left in a locked house and days later neighbours heard cries and investigated. No one ever knew what had happened to their parents. His brother, who was older and more robust, had already gone to the older children's orphanage, but Gabriel would soon be three and they feared for him as they felt he would not be able to survive in that rougher environment when he was moved there after his third birthday

Charlotte and I were very drawn to this little boy and so a few days later we went to visit him again. Charlotte saw him sitting on a potty with a row of other toddlers and said that when he looked at her she saw recognition in his eyes. Again we waited until he was brought to us – again he was put through his paces and as he was carried away I saw silent tears running down his face.

Then followed many desperate faxes to Mary. She seemed to want us to choose a girl to even up the sexes – It took a lot of prayer and more faxes sent from Onesti for her to finally change her mind and give us the go ahead to have him. It was such a relief, and filled with joy, we rang the orphanage and told them we could have him, but we were shattered next day when they rang to say we could only have Gabriel if we agreed to have his older brother as well. We put this to Mary who flatly refused.

I was distraught, like the staff I felt that he would not survive in the other orphanage and that his life was in the balance. I remembered that Mary had said that she might consider having another house, and that gave me an idea – what if I bought a house with my six thousand pounds? The houses in the village were quite basic and mostly cost about that. We did not have to make it westernised like our houses, but could keep it like the Romanian way with a couple to live there and run it.

So Charlotte and I started looking and immediately found an empty house with some land and an orchard. Then one of the helpers, with her husband, (who was our handyman), offered to move in with their two daughters and run it. That would make two adults and four children – it all began to seem possible. (In my eagerness I discounted a niggling concern about the Romanian couple, they were 7th Day Adventist and seemed a bit prejudiced and rigid in their views and unlike the rest of the staff did not seem quite so trustworthy) However we faxed Mary and told her about this idea and got an immediate reply. She was adamantly against it. She even offered to pay to fly me home to England so she could explain to me the mountain of bureaucracy and paperwork and permissions that might take years to surmount. Finally she said that she would be unable to support this venture in any way. I would be on my own.

That night was one of the saddest of my life. I really loved Gabriel and felt a desperate urge to save him. Charlotte and two friends who were staying began to point out what I would be taking on if I bought the house. So the night seemed endless as I swung from one thought to another: I could buy the house, but I did not have enough money to pay for all the food and expenses and the couples wages. (It would have to be until the boys were grown up). I felt that if I had enough faith I would go ahead in spite of that…..A 'real' Christian would not be frightened off by lack of money, they would just say "God will provide" and go ahead trustingly. But what if Mary was right and it would take so long to set up that Gabriel would have to go to the big orphanage anyway.

To and fro I swung, hating myself for my doubts, until at dawn I wrote a fax to Mary telling her not to worry, I had heard her arguments about costs and the bureaucratic difficulties involved in setting something up, and was giving up the idea. Charlotte and the two friends were very relieved when I told them, as they had become worried that I had got carried away by enthusiasm and had not considered the snags. I borrowed the jeep, and with a leaden heart – almost hating myself as a coward, I set off to Onesti to send the fax to Mary.

As I left Charlotte asked me to call at the mayor's office in the next town and give them a paper about a car. I called at the office on my way to Onesti and gave them the form and as I was leaving the phone rang and someone said that there was someone on the phone asking for me. Puzzled, I went to the phone and it was Charlotte. She said that the orphanage had just phoned to say that a Romanian Professor and his wife from Bucharest were going to adopt Gabriel and his brother immediately.

The joy and relief was almost overpowering as I drove on to Onesti to send the fax. I prayed "Thank you...thank you... thank you..." again and again.

This was SO much better than my plan. I remembered how Mary had told me that it had taken years of tackling red tape and being passed from department to department, often with months of waiting in between, before she could get her first children. But this way Gabriel and his brother would be adopted – now – and hopefully by someone intelligent and caring and become a family.

I was overawed by God's mercy and kindness. I was condemning myself for lack of faith and he just came up with a far better solution. What I had forgotten was that God also loved Gabriel and wanted the best for him. It was the most amazing relief and I was once again awed by God's timing.

CHAPTER SEVENTEEN

Charlotte and I both went home for a couple of weeks at Christmas, and I was due to return two weeks before her, but I would not be alone because Martin Simpson, an old friend, said he would come with me for a month.

January was very cold and soon after we arrived we had some deep snowfalls, but again the children got a lot of fun out of it. They were robust and hardy and we all climbed up into the hills and made snowmen and tumbled and rolled. It was so good having Martin there, though he did not speak any Romanian, he was very practical and almost immediately began splitting the vast pile of logs that would be needed for next year's heating. Also it was a relief to have him there to help if anything went wrong with the pump or generator or Land Rover in this cold weather, though luckily everything went very smoothly.

One problem did arise that he was not able to help with. Vasile got sick. I had grown very fond of Vasile. He was a very loving but quite a nervous little boy. He was as happy as anything in familiar surroundings but if we took the children into town he became quite timid and would stand behind me clutching onto my skirt and looking around my legs. Once, we had all piled into the Land Rover and gone to one of the helper's houses for a little party with her children. Vasile watched the other children playing games from the security of my lap, then he would climb down and join in for a few minutes and then rush back and scramble onto my lap until he had plucked up courage to join in again. He kept this up for the whole party – I was a sort of Granny chair.

But now he was listless and had a high temperature. There was a doctor who came to the village hall sometimes, and so I took Vasile along to see her. She examined him and decided that he should go to the Hospital. I was appalled. I had seen inside a Romanian Hospital and I felt strongly that it was the last place that he should go. He looked terrified at the idea – so I said that we would care for him at home. She then pointed out that if I took that decision I had to take full responsibility and she made me sign some papers absolving her from it. It felt very frightening. I just had time for a quick prayer asking for a clear direction to tell me if I was putting him in any danger with this decision, and then signed the papers and took him home.

He had to have an injection of antibiotics four times a day – at 6am, 12 noon, 6pm and midnight. And the nurse from the next village would come and give it to him. We made Vasile very comfortable in bed with books and toys and the only problem was his terror of the injection. I had to collect the nurse for the 6am and midnight injections, and driving along the dark snowy road under a starry sky to get her was quite beautiful.

But I was concerned that the helper on duty woke Vasile as the nurse arrived and then he had to watch her slowly getting everything ready and working himself into a crying frenzy. Finally I insisted that she did her arrangements before he was woken, so that within a few minutes of him being woken she could give it to him. This worked and he hardly had time to cry before it was all over and he was cuddled in my arms sucking a sweet and starting to drop off to sleep again. Somehow this method seemed to calm his fears generally and he managed the daytime sessions better as well. Thankfully by the time the course of injections was finished he was better, and I was so relieved I had kept him safe with us. I had such a deep instinct that to have let him go would have frightened and damaged him emotionally and undermined his trust in us.

Once someone arrived from some official department to question the children, They were asked whether they had a mother.

"No"

A father?

"No"

A Grandmother?

"Yes – Caroline is our grandmother" I was very touched.

After two weeks Charlotte returned and she and Martin became good friends, and now started a time of fun. On Sundays Martin, Charlotte and I would take bread and cheese and go off for the day, walking miles. I loved the way we could wander anywhere on these wooded hills – nothing was fenced off. Once, when we were far from home we saw a large patch of unmelted snow and leading right across it were the fresh footprints of a large bear. I remembered how one of the old ladies in the village had complained to us that she hated it when all the chained up dogs started barking at night because it meant the wolves were in the village, and I felt a sort of wonder to be here in this wild place.

A lovely girl called Fanny sometimes joined us at weekends. She had raised money to help the Harja project when Mary had visited her school to give a talk. But Fanny had not just raised money, she decided to work in Romania for her gap year before going to university and was working in a hospital in Bacau in the children's wards where she comforted and played with the children there. This hospital reminded me a little of Braila, even though conditions and bedding were much better, because here, like Braila, were children desperate for love, reaching out imploringly as you passed their cots, or just rocking in despair.

Weekends became even more fun now as Fanny, Charlotte, Martin and I all got on so well even though we were all different ages – none of us were even in the same decade. We went for long walks in the hills with the children and had picnics, and when the snow went, we made camp fires.

Martin decided to stay another month when his month was almost up so we went to the police department to see about his visa being extended.

I was quite nervous of the Romanian police. I remembered how in Braila when I went to the police department about my Romanian identity card there was some stupid problem and when I objected quite mildly, in the way one would in England, I suddenly saw the cold look in his eyes – a look so terrifying that I stopped in confusion and backed off apologising. I remembered that the Romanian police were the most oppressive in the communist block and countless people had just disappeared – these policemen in front of me were from that era – the political changes had not replaced them.

The police station in Bacau was crowded with people queuing at all the counters all patiently waiting. The only sound was the thump of rubber stamps. It took many hours going from department to department to get Martin's visa extended. Then I noticed among the crowds there were two nuns wearing long white robes edged with blue, and an inkling of memory told me that they were Mother Teresa's nuns. I checked with Charlotte when we got home she said she thought there was a convent somewhere there.

One day towards the end of my time there Charlotte said she had to go to Braila and asked whether I would go with her. It was seven months since I was last there, Charlotte had told me that she had heard an unconfirmed rumour that Alin had died. But I knew that we would not be visiting the orphanage, so with rather mixed feelings I agreed because it would be a long drive for Charlotte to have to do alone – all down the Eastern side of Romania over rough unmarked roads, (for some reason there were no road maps in Romania.)

When we got to Braila Charlotte sorted out her business and then out of curiosity we went to look at my old apartment bloc. Everything was just the same, the patch of waste ground in front of the entrance, the broken glass in the door, a few feral dogs.

Then something strange happened, one of the dogs broke away from the others and started running towards us and then I realised it was the young dog with the broken leg that Doreen and I had fed when we were last there. Amazingly it must have seen me, and somehow recognised me after all this time. And the strange thing was this was a dog I had never touched – but now it leapt around me making small whining noises in its throat, and I was able to stroke and fondle it for the first time. Then, in the matter-of-fact way dogs have – greetings over, it turned and ran back to join its pack.

Chapter Eighteen

One time – towards the end of winter, when the snow had melted and spring was waiting to come, I was woken by a sound that was completely familiar, though it felt as if it was a long time since I had heard it. I recognised it at once – it was the soft slow thud of a horse's hooves, a faint jingle of harness and a few sharp clicks as the plough nicked a stone as it cut through the earth. Rushing to the window I looked out and there below my window was an old woman leading a horse while an old man walked behind holding the plough – they had already done three rows. Standing there watching them I was puzzled at the instant familiarity of the sounds because I have no memory of where I might have heard them before.

Meanwhile Charlotte and I continued looking for the last child. This time we went to the larger town of Bacau. It was a long cold drive and we sat in an office while a social worker flicked through a list of children – for all the world like an estate agent flicking through letting properties, and just as dispassionate. Occasionally she would show us a photograph of some waif like little child and then decide that it would not be possible. The reasons were various. One lovely child was dismissed because it was a gypsy and she said its family would pester us for ever more. It was no good telling her that Vasile was a gypsy, she was already flicking through again. Then she stopped and suggested we meet a little boy who was in a nearby orphanage. He was 16 months old and had been thrown from a train at birth, in a plastic bag, complete with placenta.

So off we went to the orphanage where we were shown into a waiting room and after a lot of talk a nurse brought in a little child whose head was completely covered with a tight fitting bonnet. He was chubby and rosy cheeked and gazed around in wonder at the lights and toys, and when Charlotte showed him a toy piano that made a little flag jump up when you hit the keys – he laughed – he was quite lovely. Then we were told that though legally he had been available for adoption, in fact he was unlikely to be chosen because apparently people were put off by his history and the possibility that he might be brain damaged. But though he seemed young for his age; more like 10 months old, we both thought he was bright. He looked at a book and turned the pages. And we were both enchanted.

Then Charlotte removed the close fitting bonnet because we wondered whether it might cover any scars, but what we found was that he had red hair. It was soft and straight and the colour of autumn leaves. Charlotte pointed out to me that she had never seen anyone with red hair in Romania. We did notice the nurse seemed shocked to see we had uncovered his hair and even more surprised that we seemed to love him in spite of his hair, so Charlotte explained that lots of people had red hair where we come from, and so we did not find it a problem. We arranged to see him again next week and drove home hopeful that we might be able to have him.

Mary approved, and so the wheels of Romanian bureaucracy began to turn – medical tests, papers, forms, permissions, stamps etc etc. The next week we drove back to see him again but were told that he was in hospital with an ear infection and we could not see him, the following week when we returned there was another excuse and on the third week, when we thought we might be able to bring him home, we again set off at dawn with all sorts of warm clothes, and blankets and hot water bottles. But in the office we were told casually that he had been adopted by a Swiss adoption agency.

Driving back we wondered why they never bothered to ring us up to let us know but let us come all that way in vain, we also wondered whether our enthusiasm had surprised them and made them realise that to Western eyes he was very attractive . Charlotte also guessed that the Swiss agency had probably given them some money. So we said a prayer for the nameless little boy, that he would be adopted by a loving family and have a good life. Oddly enough, though we were sad and disappointed we felt that God was involved and everything had happened as it was meant to. Maybe our role had been to clear away some of their doubts about him.. Life is so strange sometimes.

Now I could not use my six thousand pounds to buy a house, I needed to know how to spend it wisely, and answers began to fall in place so easily that I felt that my prayers asking to be given direction were being answered.

I remembered the two elderly English ladies that Charlotte had taken me to meet. I thought about how they had struggled for years to help the children in their village, and I was touched by their unselfish devotion and the very Spartan lives they lived as every spare penny went to help others.

So I was able to give them a thousand pounds. Another three thousand went to buy a field for our two houses. I had noticed that we were the only people who had to buy everything that we ate. A field would mean that we could grow a lot of the food and preserve it for the winter in the Romanian way, and have a few chickens. It amazed me how well people seemed to manage with quite small patches of land. All our staff knew how to manage like that, and it would be something that the children could help with.

But that left two thousand. Looking back I can see that this last decision was taken completely out of my hands – It was as if it had been planned months before, but at that time I did not realise it. I was aware that my time here was coming to a close as I was due to leave just before Easter. Then suddenly I remembered the two nuns I had seen renewing their visas at the police station weeks before. I did not know anything about what they did, but felt an urgent need to find out. I did not even know what they were called or where they lived but Charlotte said she would try to find out where their convent was.

A few days later she drove me to Bacau and dropped me at the top of an unmade up street on the edge of the town. The road was full of potholes and banks of dirty snow were piled up along it. At the end was the convent surrounded by a high wall. I knocked, and a nun let me in and went to get their Principle, Sister Fabriana. The inside was quite unlike the austere exterior even though it was very simply furnished. All around were people being cared for, some in wheelchairs, some who were very disabled lying on mattresses, some being gently fed. All the people seemed handicapped in some way.

Sister Fabriana showed me around, and then we went into her office and I explained why I had come. Immediately we hit a snag, they did not have a bank account so there was no way I could get the money to them except by cash, but the money was in my bank account in England. She suggested that before I left I might like to see their chapel and she took me across the yard to a wooden building. The chapel was just a room, it was painted white so it seem full of light reflected from the snow outside. No furniture – just rush matting on the floor and a simple cross on the bare wall. We both knelt down and both had a short silent prayer. Mine was simple, something like –

"If I am to give the money to these people please make it clear to me – and make it possible."

I don't know what she prayed, but after a few minutes she got up and led the way outside. Just as we reached the door a phone started ringing in the room across the corridor and she said "Excuse me" and went to answer it.

I wandered outside where I met a little boy with no legs, and together we began playing with a plastic cup, filling it with snow and making snow castles rather like the sort of sandcastles children make on a beach. By the time Sister Fabriana came out we had a whole row of them.

Sister Fabiana smiled at me and said:

"That was Beverly Peberdy who is coming to visit us at Easter, and I said to her 'God has has sent us someone off the street to give us some money, can you bring it out to us?' And she said yes"

Problem solved. Another swift answer to a prayer.

Funnily enough I remembered the name Beverly Peberdy, because she was the lady I read about on the plane when I first came out to work in Romania fourteen months earlier. I remembered now that she had met some Mother Teresa sisters and had become a Christian. These must be the sisters she met.

So when I returned to England I immediately phoned her and was able to send a bankers draft to her bank and it cleared just in time for her to cash it before she left. While on the phone I asked her how often she rang the convent, and she said about twice a year as it was so expensive.

I pondered about how one of her twice a year calls could come within minutes of my prayer, and just before I was about to leave the convent, and had to smile at another instance of God's timing.

Chapter Nineteen

Back in Harja it was now time to leave; my year in Romania was up. Driving to the station to catch the train there were light flurries of snow – just like when I first came to live here six months before in October. But I knew that shortly the warm weather would come, and then the hot dry summer when vines would ripen and the corn grow high, and the hay on the grassy slopes would be cut with scythes and built up into stacks balanced delicately and loosely onto a tripod of fir branches where it would stay until needed. (The first time I had seen these on the hillside I had been amazed – surely they would be blown to pieces in no time – but that did not happen, and after a while I came to realise that there was so much less wind here than I was used to on the west coast of Britain).

Looking around at the now familiar countryside I realised that there had grown up a love for this country. It had crept in so gradually that I had not noticed, but I remembered how the last time I was back in Devon I had heard myself say to someone that I would be going home in a week – home!

Then during the long train ride to Bucharest I thought about this last year. Among the griefs there had been surprising patches of joy, and also as a new Christian, a confirmation that God was involved with every minute of our daily lives because every time things had seemed desperate He had been there. There had been so many instances; far more than I have mentioned here, when I had realised that something could not be explained away by coincidence. I wish I had made a note of them at the time but instead I had just said "Thank you" with a very grateful heart.

Also I was so glad that I had come to Harja and been given a chance to see another older more rural side of Romania, and my heart went out to this poor beleaguered country crawling painfully out after being crushed by forty years of Communist domination.

That had been a time when Christians were required to agree that the State was more important than God. Some people capitulated, but some refused to submit and were imprisoned indefinitely. Many died in prison, while others, like Richard Wormbrand, who was imprisoned for fourteen years, used that time to minister to his fellow prisoners. He wrote an inspiring book about how God was so closely involved with their lives there, and caused many things to happen that were unexplainable logically. He told how in one instance he was in solitary confinement and felt the need to preach. So alone in his cell he preached out loud. Years later he met a man who had been in a different prison at that time, and who had given up the will to live until he heard in his head the words that Richard Wormbrand was saying.

There were so many stories of great bravery, and also sadly some disturbing ones – when in Braila we were asked to pray for a group of Baptists in a nearby village. They had no place to meet, because though they had been given the money to buy a house they were unable to do so because the priest from the orthodox church had told his congregation that he would curse anyone who sold them a house, so no one dared.

Another, fictional story, that reflected that time of oppression, concerned an undercover prayer group who met secretly. Then one evening when they were all together, the door flew open and a policeman from the Securite strode in with his gun. Instead of arresting them all immediately, he told them that he would face the wall and count to ten and anyone could leave in that time. He began counting and a few people quickly left. When he finished counting and turned around there was a handful of people left, sitting bravely and resolutely. Then he took off his coat, put down his gun, sat down, and said cheerfully "Now that lots gone we can have a proper prayer meeting."

The final overthrow of Communism came suddenly when a pastor from a Baptist church in Timisoara was about to be arrested, but as the soldiers came to take him, his whole congregation tightly surrounded him so that the soldiers could not push through, and then amazingly, the soldiers, instead of using their weapons as expected, put them down and joined the crowd surrounding the priest........The rest is history.

Quite soon after I had come to Braila, Romania had had its first free election and we watched the results on the little black and white television in Anthea and Ionel's room. In Braila there had been so many posters for the communist party and so few for the opposition, but the ruling party lost and a new democratic President, Constantinescu was elected. We watched as he greeted the vast crowd packing the square in Bucharest. The picture was blurry and the sound was distorted and after a while we saw another, much older, man come forward to address the crowd, and then we heard an amazing thing – no speech – as in a cracked old voice he started to loudly recite something and gradually there began a great murmur of combined voices joining in and we realised it was the Lord's Prayer.

Finally I thought about the staff at Harja, many of whom had become my friends. And how, led by Charlotte, they had absorbed her values and were happy and loving and conscientious towards their charges. And Braila showed what can happen when fear and ignorance and the lack of any direction can cause such suffering both to the children, and I also realised, to the staff.

Doreen with Andra on our first visit

Our houses

Neighbours outside our houses

Elvis, Florina and Alina with helper

All the children outside the school

Picnic time

Charlotte and Ancuta

Clockwise from top left. Marius, Silviu,
Luci, Vasili and Andra

The market. Horses had to pull great weights
behind the cart to show their strength

The shepherd, (centre) in his great cloak of fleece

Me with Vasile, Martin with Florina, Charlotte with Corina

Dancing

Martin splitting logs for
next winter

Shopping   Driving the Land Rover

Getting the bread

THE BREAKTHROUGH – HOPE AT LAST

CHAPTER TWENTY

When I got back to England for the last time I began to get in touch with other people connected with Romania, and met a remarkable woman called Patty Baxter. She was strong, and warm and a great talker. She had started, and supported a project in Western Romania called Hope Romania where 10 rescued children lived like a family with Doina and Michael Nistor, their Romanian house parents.

Patty invited me to come with her on her next trip out, and so I joined her and Sally Fitzharris (who was the mother of Fanny Harris, the young friend who used to visit us in Harja). The three of us drove in a white van across Europe. We set up a sort of watch system rather like I had known sailing to The Azores and back. In rotation one drove, the other sat talking to the driver keeping her awake, while the third one lay on a mattress in the back. In this way we were able to drive non stop day and night. Patty said it was important not to stop as recently white vans had been targeted by thieves and in some cases the drivers were killed.

That time became a time of great closeness, as driving on through the night, Patty and I talked about how God had connected with our lives. She had become a deeply committed Christian as her work in Romania continued, and rather like me she felt that God was directly involved. She was a Roman Catholic and I was Anglican, but there was no difference, as again and again we found amazing parallels in our stories.

At Casa Hope we met Doina and the children. They lived in the middle of the town in a large relaxed family home. The whole project was very much connected with the life of the town, as every day food parcels were prepared for families who were in desperate need, and these were delivered by the children. There was only enough food in each parcel for that days needs, so that in some cases a drunken husband could not steal the food to buy drink. Like everything there, it was low key, simple and loving. The children in the house, who were all older than our Harja children were very involved with this work of helping others. While we were there one of them came back to say that they had found a couple where the man was injured and could not work and they were destitute. So this couple was added to the list of recipients. Some of the mothers who were being supported came into the kitchen and helped out in any way they could.

Patty had also started a bakery and a bread kitchen and had bought a farm called the Ark of Hope. Patty was the sort of person who when she saw a need she thought how best to fill it and trusted that the means to do so would be there. It must have been – and still is – an enormous responsibility to have so many people dependant on her fund raising in England.

She took us to meet one family she was helping, and so, carrying a bag of basics like bread, milk and sausage we crossed some waste ground and approached a derelict looking building. Most of the windows were gaping holes where the wood had been stripped away for firewood. We went up some stairs and into a room where there was just a table a few chairs and a bed. It was bare but very neat and clean, and on the bed were some little children sitting in a row watching us.

As we dumped the bag on the table I looked at the children and noticed that their merry little eyes were all lit up with excitement as they watched their mother unpack the food. Their eyes were so very different from the dead hopeless look of the children in Braila, and I suddenly sensed that children with a strong loving mother can survive extremes of poverty without damage. If however, that mother is forced 'for their own good' to give them up, the result is tragedy. The comparatively small outlay needed to keep a family ticking over like this is vast in terms of misery averted. I thought what a wonderful thing Patty was doing sustaining so many people in this low key way. We went out and saw the farm, and then our time was up and we drove back to England. Again it was a pleasure as the three of us felt so close.

Back home I was increasingly conscious that things in Braila were continuing in the same awful way, and I was doing nothing about it. I remembered how I had read that part of psalm 82 that seemed to be directly telling me to fight for the children. I prayed about it as I felt so helpless, and then opening the bible it fell open at the psalms, and I found myself looking at psalm 10, and read:

> But you, O God do see trouble and grief
> You consider it and take it in hand
> The victim commits himself to you:
> You are the helper of the fatherless
> Break the arm of the wicked and evil man
> Call him to account for his wickedness
> That would not be found out
> The Lord is King for ever and ever;
> You hear, O Lord, the desire of the afflicted;
> You encourage them, and you listen to their cry,
> Defending the fatherless and oppressed,
> In order that man, who is of the earth, may terrify no more.

I decided to write a report, and the next morning I woke very early and was able to scribble it down as fast as I could as the words flowed almost as if they were being dictated. I did not feel the need to change anything and was able to type it out word for word. I am convinced that I was not alone while writing this report because I believe it is clearer and more succinct than anything that I could have written.

Below is a copy of that report

THE REPORT

Almost three years ago some English girls, working in an British run hospice in Romania followed up a child that had been returned to its original orphanage in Braila, Sectia RMPSC.

Appalled at what they saw there, they offered to help. The offer was accepted and vast amounts of toys, equipment and medical supplies arrived. They set up a playroom, well equipped and with a Romanian educator. In Spring '96 two of the girls moved to Braila and worked there full time.

It was hoped that with the equipment, and their example of loving care, things might improve. I went out in January '97 to replace a girl who had married and left.

The situation was this: 47 children termed 'handicapped' were all treated as mentally deficient, whatever their problem. Apart from the playroom, all equipment sent out from England was kept in two locked rooms, packed from floor to ceiling with toys, clothes, games etc. The only benefit the children had was when we took them individually to the playroom. Their basic regime was for the older, active ones to be herded together on a mat, guarded by someone with a stick. The younger or helpless lay in wet stinking cots without bedding 24 hours a day, while the disturbed or difficult were tied up permanently.

Many of the children are of normal intelligence, their problems being physical initially: deformed hips or feet, split palate, slight cerebral palsy and four with AIDS. However, they do not learn to speak as the staff do not talk with the children, this is so firmly entrenched in the staff's minds that it causes derision when we started talking and singing to the children. In June 1997 we employed a Romanian speech therapist to help the children. She said that with just a few exceptions, most had the potential to learn to speak. When we had to leave she was prepared to work on unpaid, but was told to leave also, and has not been allowed back since the end of August 1997.

We realise that deprivation, lack of knowledge, poverty, has caused similar situations all over the world – why is this different? Because what is unacceptable, is the undercurrent of deliberate cruelty.

Instances of cruelty:

Marius arrived in the spring, like a normal three year old he liked to run around. To stop this he was tied into a chair – ironically one of the remedial chairs we had provided – his hands were tied down to the arms of the chair and a strap went around his middle to the back of the chair. His cries were ignored, until he eventually just sat silently with tears running down his cheeks. The only time he was free was when we took him down to the playroom where he played very happily and constructively with the toys.. A few minutes after returning him to the salon, he would be again tied up. By the summer he had learned to sit doing nothing like the other children and was freed.

Vasile, an intelligent boy with AIDS, tied to a chair, is slapped across the face because "He is ugly and can't feel it"

Small children are sitting on potties when we arrive at nine thirty. They stay there all morning and are even fed on them at twelve noon. As a result they get weals on their bottoms that are raised, livid and oozing. Yet fear keeps them from moving off.

Lunch is a semi-liquid mush fed from either a bottle or cup. While up to eight staff stand around chatting one member is expected to feed a room full of approximately eleven children. The children are not held while bottle fed. The bottles are propped into their moths as they lie. Many times the teats come off, or the food runs out of the large hole soaking the child's neck and back.

No notice is taken when this happens and the child is never offered replacement food or cleaned up. Any cries are ignored.

Those able to sit up are fed from a cup (these children are not shown how to feed themselves or to hold a spoon). They are fed very fast. I secretly timed how long it takes to spoon feed each child and the average was one minute forty seconds. This means that the child does not even have time to close its mouth as the sloppy mush is gulped down, if anyone gagged or slowed down the half full cup would be taken away with the comment "Oh you don't want it then" and a small grim smile as the howls of anguish broke out.

Children who are too deformed to move develop hideous bedsores. Apart from ourselves we never saw these children being turned or treated. They are in pain with the wet bedding and moan constantly. This is always ignored.

Fanica and Corina, both with normal intelligence, have deformed feet and are unable to walk. After Fanica had an operation we had remedial boots made for them which would enable them to walk. We were unable to get any member of staff to put these boots on the two girls. And when I pleaded, the next day they were on, but on the wrong children, and the following day they were on the right children but on the wrong feet. Their point made, the staff never attempted to put them on again.

Alin, aged ten, weighing just twenty four pounds had had his hands tied behind his back for so long that he held them there even when they were not tied, and when he was disturbed he cried for us to tie them. We compromised by tying them so loosely that he was able to slip a hand out if needed. He accepted this arrangement.

Conclusion

The problem is not so much specific isolated instances of cruelty, but repeated endless small cruelties going on every day, coupled with the complete absence of any warmth and affection, cause great suffering. This is reflected in the high death rate. Out of 47 children when I started seven have died. (Geta –Paval – Mona – Vasile – Adrian – Ionel – Florin) And then I heard in January '98 three more were deteriorating. Apart from the four AIDS children, these children are not officially ill in any way.

The building/staff ratio/lack of equipment/poor food are all, I suspect, standard. It is the staff's total lack of humanity towards their charges that has caused this place to be so unacceptable.

Dr. Stefan Bobecescu and the staff must be replaced, as peer pressure causes any new member of staff to conform to the status quo. It takes about a week and we have watched it happen with great sadness.

The girl I went out to help, ******, has since married a Romanian. She has been banned from the orphanage since June '97 when they tried to talk to Dr Stefan about deteriorating conditions. I worked on until September.

Now the Orphanage will not let any outsiders in. Appeals made through the local medical authorities in Braila are met with a freeze out, and the refusal to issue a renewal visa for ******, so she and her husband have had to leave for England.

THE END

I sent a copy to our Euro M.P. Graham Watson and a few other like minded people, including Patty. Patty rang and advised me to 'hold my horses' as things were a bit delicate at the moment and it might not be the right time to distribute it generally. Because of my respect for Patty I agreed to put it aside for a while, as I also was a little uneasy about what to do next.

In the meantime I felt I would like to raise some money to help Patty, but I did not know how. I hate asking people for money and apart from that I am very bad at it, so I prayed for a solution, and a few days later, as before, I had a dream.

It had the same remarkable clarity as my earlier dreams, but not their sense of danger. It was very simple; I was trying to fit animals into our Romanian Land Rover. The problem was that they were cut out animals from an enormous Noah's ark jigsaw puzzle. Then I woke up with my heart racing as I felt that it was significant.

The next morning I started to think about making a pottery Noah's ark and filling it with animals, I experimented, but nothing seemed to work until I came back to the idea of a jigsaw puzzle. So I tried rolling out a flat slab of clay and cutting it into the shape of an ark with a hole in the middle which would be filled with the flat cut out shapes of animals and birds all fitting tightly together. I drew a rough sketch of the centre rectangle and then quickly sketched the animals in. Each piece was a separate creature with no reference to scale. It went well and I managed to fit nineteen pieces together but was left with an awkward hole where the twentieth piece should be. It was a difficult little shape and I spent more time trying to find an animal that might fit it than it had taken to do all the others, but still nothing looked right.

I decided to leave it as a young friend was coming to stay the night. She, like Sam, had become a sudden and deeply committed Christian. I told her about the ark and she immediately said

"Why not a gorilla?" It was ridiculous because it was a very small space, but when she had gone I looked up gorillas in Hegner's "The Parade of the Animal Kingdom" a great tome of a book published in 1935 with 664 pages. And found that the last chapter was devoted to apes and right at the end was a photo of a gorilla and I realised that his head and shoulders exactly fitted the space. After drawing the gorilla's head from the book I looked at the last paragraph in the book and read: 'Noah must have heaved a sigh of relief when the gorilla finally entered the ark and the gangplank was hauled in' I had to laugh out loud.

I realised that making the arks would take hours of work so I advertised for volunteers to come and help with the making, and so on two mornings a week a group of ladies turned up and we got a little production line going, with everyone gradually finding a job that they were good at, and it was great fun and very companionable sitting around my kitchen table chatting and sponging the pieces smooth.

We did not know what to sell them for until I realised that 33.3 was a third of a hundred, and say we sold them for thirty five pounds each and made a limited edition of a hundred we would get the three thousand five hundred I was hoping for.

Soon the arks were good enough to sell and the team began to come up with ideas for venues, we attended various craft fairs and shows and it was great fun. We found that we could sell any spare animal pieces as fridge magnets because if one of the 20 broke it was not possible to replace it, so all nineteen were spare. It felt very blessed as they continued to sell for what was a very high price for this part of the world. Finally when the hundredth was completed we realised they had brought in six thousand pounds – I still can't quite understand how.

Early the next year I again took out the report about the Braila orphanage and had hundreds of photocopies made. This time Patty gave me her blessing and told me to go for it.

I then sent a copy with a covering letter to every bishop in the country asking for prayer (David was able to give me their addresses) and to every British Member of the European Parliament as I had heard that Romania was wanting to join the European Union and I felt our Euro MP's should know what was still happening there. Also I sent a copy to everyone else I could think of.

Then the White Cross Mission got in touch, they were a Cornish charity that had been started by the Reverend Pat Robson. They had been working with similar children in Western Romania and now had a number of rescue houses, and had a lot of experience. Pat had been sent my report by one of the Bishops. She rang to tell me that the Romanian President, Mr. Constantinescu would be coming to England in the next week and that she was due to meet him and would raise the matter with him, she also said that many of the M.E.P.s would also be present. It felt like another example of Gods practical timing and I was so grateful that I had not sent the report out generally nine months earlier.

I found Pat a great help. She was direct and unsentimental and had achieved amazing things, I met her and was able to talk to her about my worries that in publicising things, with all the best intentions in the world, I might be causing harm.

She told me that when she was at some big Romanian/Anglo reception, she was talking to a woman high up in the Romanian embassy about bringing more publicity and pressure to bear to stop the atrocities, and was told that if anything like that happened then visas would be refused and measures would be taken to put their rescue houses in jeopardy –a clear threat– Pat felt that it was because of Romanian officialdom's determination to save face. The trouble was that almost all of the people working to help in Romania have built up sanctuaries in Romania that are very vulnerable. She said that it had to be me who wrote and circulated the report because I was the only person connected with Braila who was safe from repercussions from the Romanian Government.

Both Anthea and Susan had married Romanian men who, though they were now all living in England, still had vulnerable families left in Romania and were frightened of causing trouble for them, and so did not dare say anything. And everyone else I knew who was connected to Romania had started charities or had ongoing work there that was very precious and vulnerable. They all knew that while their work was in Romania they could not afford to upset the authorities.

But I was not involved in anything that could be damaged by speaking the truth – as Pat Robson pointed out – I was a loose cannon! I could say the things that they wanted to but daren't. I was so glad that during my time in Romania I was not officially connected in any way with either of the charities I worked with, but was just there in the capacity of a volunteer.

The response from sending out the reports was encouraging – so many bishops replied with promises of prayer. and many of the Euro M.Ps also replied, (though one curious thing I noticed was that only the Labour M.Ps said they could not help as I lived outside their constituency, which seemed nonsense – what did it matter where I lived?)

Then gradually things began to happen. I had the feeling that the report was like a stone dropped in a pool and its ripples were spreading outwards.

I heard that Pat Robson had gone to Braila and was arranging to send in a speech therapist. She asked me to fund it, and I was so happy to have found a way to pass some of the money over to help my children in Braila at last.

Mary Gibson passed the report on to someone in the BBC who decided to feature it in the Nine O' Clock News, but first they sent a team to Braila to photograph the conditions for themselves. They had to get official permission and so Dr Stefan was expecting them and had put mattresses and sheets on the beds dressed the children in clean donated clothes and made every effort to show how good everything was to the visiting team. But we were able to forward some of Doreen's video footage to the BBC and were gratified to see that this was what was mainly chosen for the programme.

The European commission also visited. They were shocked by what they saw,and promised to make changes.

The charity Christian Children's Fund also offered to help. Either directly, or with prayer.

Our local Euro MP Graham Watson arranged to table a motion about it in the European parliament, but was stopped at the last moment by promises from Romania to improve things. I was sceptical about these promises at first, but though it took time, it was as if a door was opened a chink and light and air were starting to pour through.

Graham Watson and his office manager Sue Foster continued campaigning on our behalf, they never gave up. And then in May 2000 came the best news of all. I heard that in negotiations between Romania and the EU this Sectia RMPSC in Braila was mentioned specifically by name, but also it was emphasised that similar establishments would also need to be brought in line with the rest of Europe. This was more than I had ever hoped for, and it gave me great joy.

Then the Finnish Euro MP, Ms Thors, who was especially concerned with human rights and was a member of the ELDR group in Parliament became involved.

A Swiss team went to Braila to begin to help. They provided man power and experience and knowledge and started a programme whereby every week a few of the staff from Braila were sent to one of their children's centres to be trained in child care and to see how things could be done.

It took years – my input was really over with the first sending of the reports. I felt it was like passing the baton and I was deeply thankfully there were people with the expertise and ability to take it and carry it on.

Occasionally news trickled down to me. I heard that Dr Stefan and Dr Amelia had been replaced, and that now after years of speech therapy, some of the Braila children were so improved that they were able to attend a normal school, which means that not only can they speak, they must be toilet trained, properly dressed and properly fed. Things must have changed so much.

Finally I heard confirmation that this sort of thing was not just happening at Braila, but that *all* the orphanages for irrecupables were being looked into and assessed by people who were able to help them improve.

All this has been achieved by so many different people using their skills and authority.

But one thing that still fills me with wonder is the amazingly tight timing that meant that Doreen was able to come out to Braila with her cine camera and take the photos that shocked the nation and helped start the changes.

—☙ THE END ❧—

EPILOGUE

For he will deliver the needy who cry out,
The afflicted who have no one to help.
He will take pity on the weak and the needy
And save the needy from death.
He will rescue them from oppression and violence,
For precious is their blood in his sight.

Psalm 72 vv12 -14

Lightning Source UK Ltd.
Milton Keynes UK
UKOW07f1415191116

287997UK00014B/181/P

9 781786 239143